"As a world-famous athlete, with years of experience working with attorneys, agents, and money managers, it's fair to say that a few crooks and con artists have crossed my path. David Hollander is the real deal. He is a man of high honor and morality. In short, he really cares about his clients.

"I have had the great fortune of working with him over the last few years and I have seen the same passion as I had training to win medals as he does for helping people to be more empowered with their finances. Now that I am getting closer to my new 'Golden Years,' I am grateful to have worked with him on laying out a strategy to follow when it comes to my spending and income needs. If it were up to me, David would get an Olympic gold medal for that alone!"

—Kenny Harrison,
Triple Jump Hall of Fame
Olympic Gold Medalist
Current Olympic World Record
Holder

Protect Your Assets

Are You Ready for Retirement?

David Hollander, Esq.

For Sheila

TABLE OF CONTENTS

Live for Today, and Tomorrow?

Did you know more than half of all Americans accept the fact they'll have to work longer than they expected and more than one-third now believe they'll never have enough money to retire?[1] Only 54% of Generation X individuals born between 1965 and 1977 feel they're on track for a financially secure retirement, while 57% say their finances are under control.[2]

If one hopes to enjoy one's golden years of retirement, they better have the funds to do it. I have met many couples who are in their seventies and cannot retire because Social Security barely covers their health insurance premiums. The statistics above highlight the importance of developing a retirement plan that fits your specific goals so you can reduce the stresses common to retirement and enjoy the comforts you deserve.

As the founder and CEO of Liberty Group, I assist individuals and couples with their retirement planning needs.

---

[1] Jessica Dickler. CNBC. September 14, 2021. "41% of Americans say it's 'going to take a miracle' to be ready for retirement, report finds." https://www.cnbc.com/2021/09/14/36percent-of-americans-say-they-wont-have-enough-to-retire-report-finds.html

[2] Society of Actuaries. February 2022. "Generation X: Ready for Retirement?" https://www.soa.org/globalassets/assets/files/resources/research-report/2022/2022-gen-x-retirement.pdf

Among the typical services necessary to better prepare you for your future are developing effective savings strategies, protecting assets and income, and constructing a retirement plan appropriate for your age, income, and retirement dreams. Despite a general awareness among most people that retirement planning is needed, a minority actually have such a plan. And though you may be more advanced in age, designing a retirement plan is always a good idea. Retirement planning is one area where it is truly better to be late to the party than never arriving at all! If you are in your twenties or thirties and are saving now, congratulations—you have the mathematical probability of compound interest working for you!

In the following chapters of this book, several areas of retirement planning will be addressed to assist you in understanding key aspects of an effective retirement strategy. First and foremost, the assets you have already acquired must be protected, and, if possible, placed in a setting where continued growth can potentially occur. Likewise, income streams need to be positioned to provide as much possible income in retirement. With a clearer understanding of the various options available, you will be able to better participate in the planning of your retirement in conjunction with qualified retirement-planning experts. Many options exist for how to approach these goals, and each retirement plan must be individualized to your specific situation, desires, and objectives. Developing a plan to save and minimize taxation is vitally important in retirement planning, as both components are crucial for achieving success in your retirement goals. It's generally recommended to put 15% of your income toward retirement while working, but on average, employees who are fifty-five and older contribute 12.7% to a 401(k).[3]

---

[3] Cheyenne DeVon. CNBC. July 30, 2022. "Here's how much Americans have saved for retirement." https://www.cnbc.com/2022/07/30/vanguard-how-much-americans-have-saved-for-retirement-by-age.html

Similarly, many individuals lack a good understanding of the tax ramifications of various retirement investment tools, and as a result, they often "give away" a significant portion of their savings to the government. These two fundamental practices will be covered in this book in several sections so you can better appreciate their importance.

Lastly, anticipating expenses and costs in retirement can help you better predict your retirement needs, which in turn allows you to develop a more comprehensive retirement plan. Rising healthcare costs and advancing longevity both add unexpected demands on retirement income needs for many people, and carefully estimating these demands can allow you to assess whether your retirement plan will be sufficient to meet your goals. On top of longer lives and costlier healthcare, legislation and regulations related to retirement vehicles are constantly changing, as are inflationary pressures. Each of these can significantly alter the strategies you select within your retirement plan and therefore deserve your attention.

Because the scope of this book doesn't allow for descriptions of such aspects beyond introductory detail, and since no one can predict the future, you are naturally encouraged to seek concurrent expert advice about your retirement planning while investing in ongoing education about future changes. However, this book will serve to provide you with a strong foundation upon which you can further your knowledge and understanding about various retirement options. As an attorney well versed in elder law and estate planning, the head of a dually registered broker-dealer, and a financial and investment advisor, I have a comprehensive background from which I can offer sound retirement planning advice. As you proceed through the following chapters, use this information to help you in your discussions with your professional advisor in creating a retirement plan. Above all, commit to developing a retirement plan. A retirement dream without a plan is like driving cross country without a map. If you want to reach your goals successfully, making a plan for your retirement is almost always essential, no matter how old you are. You do not want to be eighty and broke.

CHAPTER 1

Getting Started — Retiring in Style

The most important question about retirement is how can you retire comfortably without running out of money along the way. Unfortunately, many people really have no concept of what their spending needs might be during retirement or how much they might need in retirement income. Some factors are more predictable than others in determining this figure. For example, anticipating future spending can be based on current expenditures to a great extent. But how do you anticipate inflation, recessions, and unexpected healthcare costs? If you have not thought about these potential setbacks, then your retirement savings may last a much shorter period of time than you thought.

Consider a client of mine, John, who retired in 2007 at the age of sixty-five. With a retirement sum of $550,000, John had begun taking out 5% of his savings annually, but unfortunately his nest egg suffered a huge hit with the most recent recession. By 2009, his retirement accounts had taken a 40% hit, and combined with his retirement withdrawals, his balance had fallen to $280,000. With an annual need of $25,000 a year, the chance John would run out of money prematurely was extremely high. And with a reduced amount of principal in his accounts, the potential for investment growth was similarly declining. Despite John's dedicated efforts to save for retirement, his strategy and plans fell short because he had failed to define his retirement goals accurately.

Recent studies by Morningstar suggest that an annual retirement withdrawal of 3.3% of your portfolio may be more accurate than the popular "4% rule."[4] It is important to keep in mind that an increase in annual withdrawals above 3% results in increasingly higher rates of retirement failures. Several factors account for this, including inflation, rising healthcare costs, and increasing longevity. The odds that at least one member of a sixty-five-year-old couple will live to ninety-three are 50%, and there is a 25% chance at least one of them will reach age ninety-seven.[5] In essence, this means one of those two individuals will need retirement funds for twenty-eight years!

Long-term care alone has witnessed a staggering surge in costs over the past few decades. In California, the median costs for a semi-private room in a nursing home facility is well over $9,000 a month.[6] Successful retirement begins with successful retirement planning, and successful planning demands an effort to be informed about your future needs. In this chapter, I will provide the tools for a retirement strategy specific to your needs, which will allow you to move in that direction.

Defining Your Goals and Needs of Retirement

How do you know how much you should save? A better question might be what are your spending needs now? You would be amazed at the percentage of people who have little

---

[4] Greg Iacurci. CNBC. November 11, 2021. "Experts say the 4% rule, a popular retirement income strategy, is outdated."
https://www.cnbc.com/2021/11/11/the-4percent-rule-a-popular-retirement-income-strategy-may-be-outdated.html
[5] Fidelity.com. February 2023. "Longevity and retirement"
https://www.fidelity.com/viewpoints/retirement/longevity
[6] Genworth.com. Genworth Cost of Care Survey: Median Cost Data Tables. January 31, 2022. https://www.genworth.com/aging-and-you/finances/cost-of-care/cost-of-care-trends-and-insights.html

knowledge about their current expenditures. Without this knowledge, predicting financial needs during retirement is impossible. This information is crucial in determining how much you should save, when you can retire, and the annual percentage allocation you can take during retirement. Therefore, the starting point for effective retirement planning involves a detailed look at your spending needs.

By taking the time to identify your expenses now, as well as those needed at retirement, you can develop an accurate retirement strategy. You will not only understand more clearly how much you currently spend, but you will also gain some perspective on what is important for your retirement. These insights will allow you to better determine your specific goals for the future.

As an example of the importance of understanding expenditures and retirement goals, another client, who lives in one of the premier areas of California, recently lost her husband unexpectedly. Despite retirement savings of $1 million, she rapidly found herself in a distressing financial situation. Though she was able to take her husband's Social Security income, she lost his pension since it was not transferrable to the spouse. She was also upside down in her home, leaving her with a hefty monthly mortgage payment. When all was said and done, she was withdrawing 8% of her retirement savings each year in order to maintain her lifestyle! In counseling her, the first step involved defining her expenditures and assets so rational decisions could be made. As a result, she made the decision to sell her home and downsize to a smaller one so she could maintain a lifestyle that would suit her needs for the duration of her retirement.

In addition to defining expenditures and assets more precisely, a second goal of retirement planning involves minimizing the amount of income taxes you are paying. After all, for every dollar saved from income tax, you have additional money to spend in retirement! Unfortunately, many individuals receive isolated advice when it comes to retirement. For example, some financial planners tend to focus on investments, while accountants tend to focus on taxes and tax planning. If these advisors fail to communicate effectively with one another, or you lack the ability to properly connect the dots, the outcome often results in lost money. No matter who you are, this is certainly not a primary goal for retirement.

A highly intelligent businessperson approached me not long ago asking for assistance with his financial planning. In reviewing his portfolio, I noted he had only six years before he was required to withdraw a disbursement from his individual retirement account (IRA). This disbursement is known as the required minimum distribution, or RMD. This gentleman, seventy-three and single, possessed a substantial IRA worth millions of dollars, necessitating the withdrawal of their Required Minimum Distribution (RMD) as taxable income. The RMD amount is calculated by dividing the IRA balance as of December 31 of the previous year by a life expectancy factor, which in this case is 26.5, based on the individual's age and marital status. Assuming the IRA was valued at $5 million, his RMD would amount to approximately $188,680.[7] And guess what? All of this money would be taxed as income at a high tax rate! As a managing partner of a major brokerage firm, he had ample resources to hire one of the highest paid accountants in the area to complete his taxes, but his accountant had not bothered to examine anything beyond the scope of this client's regular annual income. Likewise, he had failed to communicate with any of this client's other professionals.

From a broader perspective, and with detailed knowledge

---

[7] Internal Revenue Service. March 14, 2023. " Retirement Plan and IRA Required Minimum Distributions FAQs."
https://www.irs.gov/retirement-plans/retirement-plans-faqs-regarding-required-minimum-distributions#:~:text=Generally%2C%20a%20RMD%20is%20calculated,Individual%20Retirement%20Arrangements%20(IRAs).

of law, taxes, and financial investments, my advice for this client was to begin taking distributions now and invest them in a few tax-free retirement options. This would still allow his savings to grow yet avoid some of the taxation penalties down the road. In this particular case, the client had ample retirement savings to support his anticipated lifestyle after retirement, and so he would have been comfortable in retirement regardless. But no one wants to simply give away money to taxes when more attractive options exist. For this reason, a universal goal of retirement planning involves minimizing income taxation.

Another goal of retirement planning involves properly distributing your wealth to others. Ensuring your children or spouse receive a portion of your wealth might be especially important to you, or you might wish to leave a portion of your estate to a charity. If you fail to recognize these as important personal goals, serious misfortunes can result. In some scenarios, savings can be subject to excessive taxation through estate taxes, dramatically reducing the amount distributed to your heirs. In other instances, the money may be awarded to individuals for whom you had no intention of receiving your unused savings and assets. Once again, poor planning can result in major catastrophes.

For example, a couple living in New York had taken the effort to ensure that the husband's IRA, which was worth several hundred thousand dollars, would be left to their children as beneficiaries in the event both passed away. Sadly, the husband lost his wife to cancer a few years later, and the IRA remained unchanged in terms of the beneficiary designation. Eventually, the man remarried. Upon his death, the children presumed they would be entitled to the remaining retirement savings as outlined in the IRA beneficiary agreement. However, in the state of New York, the spouse is considered the beneficiary of all retirement accounts. Despite fighting the battle in court, the children lost the case as well as a substantial amount of money.

Certainly, in the preceding example, the elderly couple had the best intentions in distributing their savings to their children, and they even took steps toward that effect. Where they made a mistake was in failing to have their beneficiary forms reviewed by an attorney who knew New York state law. Once again, a disconnect between financial planning and other areas relevant to retirement occurred. Just as accountants may fail to understand financial planning, financial planners may fail to understand legal ramifications of various actions. In order to achieve your goals for retirement, multiple sources of information will likely be needed, and the use of experts who collaborate with one another about your specific needs is crucial to your retirement success.

Recently, I was speaking with a Super Bowl football champion about financial planning and retirement. From his perspective, he believed the lack of routine participation in financial planning among some members of the African American community stems from a constant inability among minority families to save money. As soon as money earned came through the door, it was immediately spent.

Saving and planning are habits that can be learned in any income bracket. While social and economic factors affect many individuals, I believe each of us has a responsibility to plan for their future; more importantly, as parents, I believe we have a responsibility to educate our children about saving and financial planning as well. By committing to a retirement plan, seeking professional advice, and demonstrating saving behaviors, the ability to enjoy a happy and comfortable retirement will be markedly increased. In addition, these positive behaviors will be passed along to future generations.

Rethinking Retirement Income Opportunities

A long time ago, a wise man once told me I should rethink the way I categorize investment options for retirement. He described four types of money which can be pursued, and some options are vastly preferable to others. The first type involves free money. What could be better than free money? Free money is simply money you collect from doing absolutely nothing. Examples of free money include winning the lottery, receiving a financial gift, or collecting an inheritance. An argument could be made in each case that the effort required to buy the lottery ticket or to endear yourself to family accounts for some value, but the bottom line is any effort in gaining those types of fortunes was minimal at best. Free money *also* includes employer-matched retirement funds. If your employer matches up to 4% of your salary and you choose to put in only 2%, then in essence you failed to receive an additional 2% in your retirement account from your employer. If your annual salary is $50,000, then you just missed an opportunity for $1,000 a year in free money.

The second-best type of money is tax-free money. Tax-free money represents money you earned; however, it avoids income tax. This means you receive 100% of the revenues! Unfortunately, I see people fail to take advantage of these investment opportunities when they clearly have important advantages. Examples of tax-free money include money invested in Roth IRAs, which can be withdrawn tax-free during retirement if working within the guidelines of these accounts. Similarly, municipal bonds also offer tax-free income withdrawals. Lastly, unique financial products like Fixed Indexed Universal Life (FIUL) insurance permits investment growth with the opportunity to withdraw money through loans from the policy without tax penalties. Each of these products will be discussed in greater detail in subsequent chapters, but it is important for you to appreciate their potential benefits in seeking to maximize retirement income opportunities in a tax-free manner.

Moving down the spectrum from most favorable to least favorable ways to create retirement income, tax-deferred money offers the next best option. Tax-deferred investments represent the more traditional retirement options, such as individual retirement accounts, annuities, and stocks (not including dividends). The money invested in these resources grows tax deferred, allowing growth to be compounded with interest over time, which usually results in larger gains. However, whenever the money is withdrawn from these accounts, it is taxed as income according to your income-tax bracket at the time. These withdrawals may be voluntary or in some cases required (as in the case of RMD associated with IRA accounts). If the growth within tax-deferred accounts is reasonable, these options remain excellent sources of retirement income for many individuals.

Lastly, taxable money represents the least attractive income source for retirement. This does not necessarily mean these options are to be avoided, since investment growth and differential tax rates may favor the use of these investments for some. Examples of taxable money include normal income from full- and part-time work, but they also include corporate bonds, stock dividends, interest on savings accounts, and capital gains made on real estate sales. These sources of money are typically taxed during the year in which the income was made, which distinguishes them from tax-deferred monies. Depending on your specific financial situation, taxable income options can still offer some advantages, especially when combined with other investment categories.

After reading the different types of ways to create retirement income, an easy conclusion would be that one should only pursue tax-free monies (since pursuing free money only can frequently be a disappointing venture). But while tax-free money is certainly better than tax-deferred and taxable monies from a purist's perspective, another important rule to retirement investing strategies is diversification. Diversification spreads your wealth so that a single misfortune does not sink your ship. Even Warren Buffet and Peter Lynch took financial hits along the way. Diversification prevents such hits from having a broad, adverse impact on your retirement plans, since in most cases some sources of income will be protected while others may not be. Therefore, despite clear advantages of tax-free monies over tax-deferred and taxable options, you may choose to have some or all of these types as part of your diversification strategy.

In the chapters to follow, diversification strategies will be discussed in detail in addition to specific sources of retirement income. Examples of various types of income can include real estate, which refers to your home as well as rental properties and other land investments. Likewise, annuities, stocks, bonds, and business royalties provide other options of income in retirement to be considered. Traditional pensions, retirement accounts, and Social Security income are of course important, and many individuals choose part-time employment for income for a multitude of reasons. As a result, there are several options for retirement income, and each source may have advantages and disadvantages depending on your specific situation. As you delve deeper into these retirement strategies, you will realize not only the importance of prioritizing income options and pursuing diversification, but also the value of seeking information, planning, and strategizing.

A Word about Hiring a Financial Advisor

In the examples of clients provided in this chapter, poor financial or tax advice has been demonstrated despite the fact that these individuals had high-priced advisors. In many other instances, individuals forego advice altogether assuming things will simply fall into place. The problem with both of these approaches stems from a failure to value assets and savings to the degree they should be valued. On the one hand, you would not want to entrust your life's savings to just anyone, and alternatively, ignoring your retirement assets is a near guarantee to fail in achieving your goals. Developing a retirement plan and strategy, being informed, and seeking help from professionals are important. In fact, hiring a financial advisor can be one of the most important decisions of your life.

With this in mind, what is the best way to find a financial advisor who can meet your retirement needs? Many of the mistakes I routinely see in this area relate to the fact that we are all extremely busy. Life gets in the way of spending the effort needed to find the right person. As a result, you might sign up for the first financial advisor interviewed, or you might fail to perform your due diligence by pursuing references and background checks. You may simply choose an advisor based on the recommendation of a family member or friend, or, even worse, you may choose a family member or friend as your advisor. While some people get lucky with this type of financial roulette, the majority end up with unsatisfactory experiences and poor results. Choosing a financial advisor is not a task where shortcuts should be taken.

A suitable financial advisor should first and foremost openly communicate with clients to collaboratively develop a sound, long-term retirement plan. Just as important, the advisor you select should work closely with tax and legal consultants concerning your retirement strategies, since each of these areas interconnect. Speaking from personal experience, my knowledge of law, taxes, and financial planning has allowed me to better serve numerous clients simply because of my enhanced ability to put the pieces of the puzzle together. In seeking the best advisor for your situation, you should interview several and explore their levels of experience. You should also investigate their participation with regulatory agencies and discuss in detail how they will communicate with other professionals when developing a solid retirement strategy for you. Using these strategies while selecting a financial advisor allows you to align yourself with a quality professional who places your needs first.

One last comment about hiring a financial advisor involves cost. Too frequently people avoid spending money on financial consulting, which makes little sense. Your retirement income and savings represent your livelihood for a significant portion of your life and possibly your children's lives. Doesn't it seem logical that you should invest money now into educating yourself about different retirement strategies from experts in the field, so you will hopefully end up with more later? Likewise, pricing for these consultants should not replace detailed research to find the most qualified financial advisor for you. Cheap often implies cheap, and pricey is not a consistent indicator of quality. Invest in the financial advisor who has the best profile based on your due diligence and remain an active participant in your retirement planning. By making these efforts, your long-term satisfaction will be much more likely, and the money spent will have been wisely invested.

CHAPTER 2

Common Retirement Options: Pensions, IRAs, and 401(k)s

Not long ago, people would leave school to work for a corporation, and in many cases, they would stay with that corporation for most (if not all) of their careers. Such occurrences are nearly unheard of today. Most employees would enjoy company pension plans for their retirement. Pension plans were ideal retirement vehicles for employees in the sense that the employees were not required to contribute any of their earned income to the pension fund. Yet upon retirement, they would receive a defined income based on their salary and longevity with the company. Though they had no say in how this money could be invested or managed, employees enjoyed a "free ride" on their employer's contributions.

Many things have changed since then. In the 1980s, several corporate scandals served to squander pension funds, leaving many people without any retirement income at all. These events led to the Employment Retirement Income Security Act, as well as the Pension Benefit Guarantee Corporation (PBGC), which now insures pensions up to a certain value amount. At the same time, employers realized the sizable costs and liabilities of managing such retirement plans. As a result, they began shifting the burden of retirement savings onto the individual through the 401(k), 403(b), or 457. Though pensions are still present today, they are much less common than they were previously.

Today, most retirement investment decisions require you to determine how much you should save, how your money will be managed, which retirement strategies are best for you, and how you can best reduce unwanted tax effects. Several options exist depending on your specific situation, and knowing the facts about each one is important in making wise retirement decisions. In this chapter, we will cover not only pensions but also individual retirement accounts (IRAs) and 401(k) plans. With this knowledge, you will be better prepared to take charge of your retirement strategies.

Pensions

Benefit plans come in two types. One type is the traditional company pension where the defined benefit is usually based on an employee's longevity at the company and their income level. The other type is a cash balance plan that is not based on those factors. Instead, a cash balance plan involves the employer placing an amount equal to a percentage of your salary (often 5%) into a credit account and allowing it to grow at a fixed interest rate. Common to both types is the employer's sole responsibility for doing all the investing while you simply show up for work! You do not contribute any of the deposits into these accounts, and the employer is responsible for ensuring the money is available for you when you retire.[8]

Unfortunately, most private companies no longer offer these types of retirement packages. Only 4% of private sector workers have a defined benefit pension plan by itself, while 14% of private companies offer a combination of both types.

---

[8] U.S. Department of Labor. "Types of Retirement Plans."
https://www.dol.gov/general/topic/retirement/typesofplans

In contrast, 84% of state and local government organizations offer traditional pensions.[9] Unlike private companies, which are moving away from these retirement options due to costs and liabilities, governments have held onto these structures in part due to the risk of change. Can you imagine being the politician running on a platform stating they would eliminate employee pension plans? The chances of reelection would not be very high.

In addition to how benefits are calculated, pensions and cash balance plans differ in another important way. Pensions traditionally require an employee to be vested in the plan over a number of years (often five years or more). Once you are vested, you may then receive all the pension funds upon retirement. While some pension plans allow you to begin taking out withdrawals at fifty-five years of age upon retirement, others require you to be sixty-five years of age. Cash balance plans likewise require you to reach retirement age before being able to withdraw funds. However, cash balance funds can be taken out earlier and rolled into another type of retirement plan (like an IRA), while pension funds cannot. Thus, while cash benefit plans often have lower retirement income payouts in comparison to pensions, they are more flexible in their management.

The value of defined benefit plans is their ability to grow tax-deferred over the course of your employment from money your employer provides. Likewise, the fixed payout you will receive upon retirement should be consistently evaluated, annually providing you a realistic perspective of your actual retirement income.

NOTE: When you are provided with a life-only option, make sure you evaluate *all* your choices critically, as a decision to take

---

[9] CNN Money. 2021. "Ultimate guide to retirement." https://money.cnn.com/retirement/guide/pensions_basics.moneym ag/index7.htm?iid=EL

100% payout for your life could end up hurting your spouse or loved ones if you die unexpectedly. That is because any unpaid portion of your original lump sum will go to the insurance company and not your beneficiary! Of course, as these monies are withdrawn, they will be subject to ordinary income taxes. However, the ability to acquire retirement income at the expense of your employer remains highly advantageous. For those of you who have this option, defined benefit plans can be a nice addition to a diversified retirement strategy.

401(k)s and Defined Contribution Plans

Like defined benefit plans, defined contribution plans (including 401(k)s) are retirement plans sponsored by employers. However, unlike defined benefit plans, these plans require contributions primarily from employees, thus placing the responsibility of saving on you. Three types of defined contribution plans exist: 401(k) plans (plans offered by private corporations to their own employees), 403(b) plans (plans offered by public educational institutions and nonprofit organizations), and 457 plans (plans offered to employees of state and municipal entities as well as some qualified nonprofit organizations). By far, the most common defined contribution plans are 401(k)s. For those who are curious, the names of 401(k), 403(b), and 457 plans reference the tax-code regulation sections that created them.

In essence, you decide how much money you wish to contribute to your 401(k). This money is contributed as pre-tax dollars and allows tax-deferred over time, making it an excellent way to secure a retirement income. In some cases, employers will offer to match employee contributions up to a certain percentage of their salary. While the money you contribute is earned money, the contribution matched by your employer is free money! Remember, nothing is better than free money.

The challenge with 401(k) plans rests on the fact that you are in charge. Upon enrolling in an employer's 401(k) plan, you have the option of investing in mutual funds, exchange-traded funds, stocks, and/or bonds. Of course, when you initially enroll, you likely select the best performing funds at the time. But this changes every year. If you are like most hard-working people, keeping up with this information is difficult. Stocks over time have offered the best return.[10] Therefore with a long-term investment in a 401(k), choosing stocks over bonds may be attractive to you. However, stocks generally have a higher risk profile, meaning that you could experience more volatility and panic when the market is down, thus losing principal. If you choose stocks, realize that you are investing over the long term and you are buying at highs and lows to even out the ride.

Other reports have shown that passively aligning your 401(k) investing strategies with the S&P 500 index generally outperforms actively managed accounts 80% of the time.[11] Likewise, choosing a large-cap mutual fund option is typically less expensive than small-cap funds in regard to management fees.[12]

Such information about your specific 401(k) funds can be easily accessed by asking the 401(k) account manager. In fact, employers are legally required to provide this information to you.

---

[10] Thomas Smith. Investopedia. June 22, 2022. "Why Stocks Generally Outperform Bonds."
https://www.investopedia.com/articles/basics/08/stocks-bonds-performance.asp#:.
[11] Greg Iacurci. CNBC. March 21, 2022. " Odds are, you're better off buying an index fund. Here's why."
https://www.cnbc.com/2022/03/21/why-index-funds-are-often-a-better-bet-than-active-funds.html
[12] Kent Thune. The Balance. March 2, 2022. "Basics on Mutual Fund Fees, Loads, and Expenses."
https://www.thebalancemoney.com/basics-on-mutual-fund-fees-loads-and-expenses-2466616#:~: 5

For many people, overseeing their 401(k) effectively causes significant stress or just does not happen because we are all busy. One effective alternative, which many employers now offer, includes a self-directed investment option wherein you are able to have an outside advisor manage your company 401(k).

In 2006, the Pension Protection Act was passed, and this legislation (among other things) gave employees greater choices in managing their retirement accounts.[13] This trend, in addition to companies wishing to reduce their liability for poor fund management, gave birth to the self-directed 401(k) option. This option allows you to move your 401(k) from the employer-sponsored manager to an advisor of your choice who can provide you with specific professional advice and typically many more investment choices. Currently about 40% of private companies offering 401(k) plans for their employees have a self-directed option which may provide you better direction according to your specific needs.[14]

Most importantly, you must actually contribute to your 401(k) in order for it to benefit your retirement. Certainly, contributing enough to maximize any employer-matched contributions is paramount, but striving to invest 10% or more from each paycheck into your 401(k) should be your goal. As of 2023, you can put up to $22,500 a year into your 401(k) if you are under fifty years of age; if you are over fifty years of age, an additional $7,500 can be contributed as well.[15] These

---

[13] Denise Appleby. Investopedia. December 11, 2021. "The Pension Protection Act of 2006—and How It Still Helps Retirement." https://www.investopedia.com/articles/retirement/06/ppa2006.asp #toc-1-improved-funding-for-defined-benefit-pension-plans
[14] Renée Pastor. CNBC. March 9, 2021. "Op-ed: Here's how to capitalize on a self-directed brokerage account within your 401(k) plan." https://www.cnbc.com/2021/03/09/how-to-capitalize-on-a-self-directed-brokerage-account-within-a-401k.html
[15] IRS. November 21, 2022. "Taxpayers should review the 401(k) and IRA limit increases for 2023."

pre-tax investments are allowed to grow tax-deferred and without penalty as long as you withdraw your retirement income after the age of fifty-nine-and-a-half years. Early withdrawals result in a 10% taxation penalty in addition to regular income taxes, unless the withdrawal is for college expenses, excessive medical expenses, first-time home purchases, sudden disability costs, or using Internal Revenue Code 72-T. Therefore, early withdrawal is discouraged in most instances.[16]

Overall, 401(k) plans are excellent retirement vehicles to be included in your diversified retirement plan. Maximizing contributions and choosing the best investment strategies for you are important. In addition, focus less on the performance index comparisons and assets under management size. Instead, if you are within ten years of retirement, identify the amount of income the plan could generate for you during your retirement years. This aspect of 401(k) plans is important to retirement success and can help you make wise decisions along the way.

Individual Retirement Accounts (IRAs)

Traditional IRA

Just as the name implies, IRAs are "individual" retirement strategies (most of the time) whereas direct benefit plans and direct contribution plans are employer-based plans in which all the employee funds are lumped into one plan. Four main types of IRAs exist: traditional IRAs, Roth IRAs, SIMPLE IRAs, and SEP IRAs. Except for Roth IRAs, all other IRA types are tax-

---

https://www.irs.gov/newsroom/taxpayers-should-review-the-401k-and-ira-limit-increases-for-2023#:

[16] Brian Baker. Bankrate. June 12, 2023. "8 ways to take penalty-free withdrawals from your IRA or 401(k)."

https://www.bankrate.com/retirement/ways-to-take-penalty-free-withdrawals-from-ira-or-401k/

deferred, meaning they are taxed as ordinary income when you withdraw funds. Some are more flexible in terms of withdrawal allowances and in requirements for distribution withdrawals. The specific aspects of each plan often determine which IRA may be best for you, along with tax effects, income levels, and employment situations.

Traditional IRAs are funded with earnings, which could be tax deductible depending on earnings and whether you have other retirement plan options. However, if you have a 401(k) or some other workplace retirement plan, contributions are only fully deductible if you fall within certain income levels. For 2023, if you are covered by a retirement plan at work, your deduction for contributions to a traditional IRA is reduced (phased out) if your modified AGI is more than $116,000 but less than $136,000 for a married couple filing a joint return, or more than $73,000 but less than $83,000 for an individual. [17]

For traditional IRAs that meet these requirements, untaxed dollars are allowed to grow tax-deferred, including all interest, dividends, and capital gains throughout the life of the plan. Anyone who earns a taxable compensation is eligible for establishing a traditional IRA on their own through a brokerage company. Individuals less than fifty years of age can contribute up to $6,500 annually into an IRA, and for those age fifty and older, up to $7,500 can be contributed.[18] Upon withdrawal, assuming you are age fifty-nine-and-a-half years or older, the money taken is subject to income tax at your current tax rate. Withdrawals before this age are still subject to the same income tax but are also generally subject to an

---

[17] IRS. "2023 IRA Deduction Limits – Effect of Modified AGI on Deduction if You Are Covered by a Retirement Plan at Work." https://www.irs.gov/retirement-plans/2023-ira-deduction-limits-effect-of-modified-agi-on-deduction-if-you-are-covered-by-a-retirement-plan-at-work
[18] IRS, "Retirement Topics – IRA Contribution Limits." https://www.irs.gov/retirement-plans/plan-participant-employee/retirement-topics-ira-contribution-limits

additional 10% tax penalty for early withdrawal. Only in instances where the money is used for college expenses, excessive medical expenses, sudden disability, a first-time home purchase, or Rule 72-T can this additional tax be avoided.[19]

In addition to potential early withdrawal penalties, traditional IRAs also have a Required Minimum Distribution (hereinafter "RMD"). Generally must start taking withdrawals from your traditional IRA, SEP IRA, SIMPLE IRA, and retirement plan accounts when you reach age seventy-two (or seventy-three if you reach age seventy-two after December 31, 2022). If you should fail to take out the RMD at that point, you will receive a tax penalty equal to 25% of the RMD value![20] The RMD is determined by formulas which consider your IRA account balance(s), your age, and your spouse's age. Thus, these RMD amounts are specific to your unique situation. Because IRA withdrawals are taxed at your current tax rate, individuals who expect lower income levels over time may prefer this retirement vehicle if they qualify.

Roth IRA

In contrast to traditional IRAs, Roth IRAs are funded with post-tax dollars which are not tax deductible. Contributions to Roth IRAs grow tax-free over time; on withdrawal, these monies are not taxed. With this in mind, individuals who expect higher incomes over time (and therefore higher income tax rates) may prefer a Roth IRA since the money contributed would be taxed on the front end instead of the back end. In addition, any actual contributions (not the interest gained) can be withdrawn from

---

[19] IRS. "Retirement Topics – Exceptions to Tax on Early Distributions." https://www.irs.gov/retirement-plans/plan-participant-employee/retirement-topics-tax-on-early-distributions
[20] IRS. "Retirement Plan and IRA Required Minimum Distributions FAQs." https://www.irs.gov/retirement-plans/retirement-plan-and-ira-required-minimum-distributions-faqs

a Roth IRA anytime. Earnings on contributions taken out prior to age fifty-nine-and-a-half years, however, would be subject to a 10% tax penalty. Likewise, in order to avoid tax penalties on withdrawal of earnings after age fifty-nine-and-a-half years, you must have been contributing to your Roth IRA account for at least five years.

For 2023, the annual contribution limits for Roth IRAs are $6,500 for individuals younger than age fifty and $7,500 for those fifty years and older. However, only certain individuals are eligible for Roth IRAs. Those who qualify to contribute the full amount must have a MAGI under $228,000 if married or under $153,000 if single.[21] Also, Roth IRAs have no RMDs during your lifetime, but your heirs must generally take them.[22] These features make the Roth IRA more flexible in comparison to traditional IRAs, but tax strategies, income levels, and plans for early withdrawal must be considered in determining which retirement option is best for you.

SIMPLE and SEP IRAs

Two other IRAs are worth mentioning, and these include SEP IRAs and SIMPLE IRAs. SEP IRAs are for self-employed individuals and small business owners. Unlike traditional and Roth IRAs, these are not technically "individual" retirement plans since the business actually makes contributions on behalf of the employee. These contributions are made with pre-tax dollars, and business owners under the age of fifty can contribute up to 25% of their income or a maximum amount

---

[21] Arielle O'Shea and Andrea Coombes. Nerdwallet. June 16, 2023 "Roth IRA Contribution and Income Limits 2023."
https://www.nerdwallet.com/article/investing/roth-ira-contribution-limits#:.
[22] Jean Folger. Investopedia. May 25, 2023. "Roth IRA Required Minimum Distributions (RMDs)."
https://www.investopedia.com/roth-ira-required-minimum-distribution-rmd-4770561

of $66,000 annually—whichever is less.[23] These types of IRAs do not have to be funded every year, allowing business owners to vary their contributions annually. Withdrawals from these accounts are taxed just as traditional IRAs are taxed and are subject to the same penalties and restrictions.

SIMPLE IRAs are also for small business owners who generally have fewer than 100 employees earning at least $5,000 a year. No other retirement plan can be in place, and the employer is required to match employee contributions dollar for dollar into the IRA up to 3% of the employee's salary—or the employer contributes a flat 2% of the employee's pay regardless of employee contributions. The benefit of the SIMPLE IRA is the increased contribution limits. Employees can contribute up to $15,500 per year if younger than fifty years of age, and this increases to $19,000 per year if fifty years and older.[24] For a single business owner who is the only employee, a SIMPLE IRA is attractive because of the matching component of the business. For some small businesses with several employees, the lower matching requirement might be attractive in comparison to other retirement plan options. Monies withdrawn from SIMPLE IRAs again follow the same rules as traditional IRAs.[25]

Getting the Guidance You Need

Traditional retirement plan options have changed a great deal over the last twenty years. Employers and corporations have shifted the responsibility of retirement saving and planning onto the employee as a means to reduce liability as well as costs. While this has provided you with greater control and oversight of your money, the complexities of many of these

---

[23] James Royal. Bankrate. November 4, 2022. "SEP IRA vs SIMPLE IRA: How they compare." https://www.bankrate.com/retirement/sep-ira-vs-simple-ira/
[24] Ibid.
[25] Ibid.

plans can make it difficult to know what is best for your particular situation.

Understanding the retirement plan your employer provides, as well as your other retirement options, allows you to make better decisions about your money. First and foremost, you should commit to making regular contributions to a retirement plan, and if your employer offers matching funds, maximizing this source of free money is extremely important. Secondly, focus more on the amount of income your plan could generate for you in retirement rather than on annual balances and rates of return. The former is what matters most when it comes to successful retirement planning. If you have any questions or need guidance from a qualified professional, I encourage you to visit our firm's website at LibertyGroupLLC.com. It's your money, after all, and you owe it to yourself to have a solid understanding of how your retirement plans are working for you.

CHAPTER 3

Stocks, Bonds, and Annuities

What happens if you max out your annual contributions to your IRA and still want to put some money away for your later years? Which option offers the best growth potential, the lowest tax penalties, and the least amount of risk? These are loaded questions with answers depending greatly on your individual situation. In choosing among your options, you should consider investments in stocks, bonds, mutual funds, and annuities. Each of these offers retirement strategy advantages and disadvantages, and understanding the pros and cons can help you make wise investment decisions.

As previously noted, you should take a diversified approach to retirement planning and investing. Diversification can reduce your level of risk when times are bad yet still offers potential for growth. Stocks, bonds, and annuities are ways in which you can diversify your retirement investments and, in many cases, complement your other retirement strategies. In this chapter, these investment options will be discussed in relation to retirement planning so you can appreciate whether these options might benefit your goals and objectives. Though some of the concepts may be complex at times, having a better understanding of these investment options allows you to make more informed decisions while asking the right questions of your professional advisor.

Stocks

Most people have at least a basic understanding of what stocks represent. In essence, stocks provide you with a stake in a company and a partial claim to the earnings of that company. Once you have decided to purchase stock in a company, you can earn income from that stock through one of two ways. You can either earn money by selling the stock if the stock has increased in value, or a company may pay out dividends periodically to investors like yourself. In both instances, the money initially invested hopefully provides positive earnings, which will provide additional income for you in retirement. Unfortunately, stocks can also lose value over time, resulting in capital losses instead of gains. Therefore, how you approach your investment in stocks is particularly important when maximizing your earning potential for retirement.

Historically, investments in stocks have produced larger gains than any other asset class, including bonds, annuities, and cash equivalents. The Standard & Poor's 500 average of annualized returns since it began in 1928 through December 31, 2022 is 9.82%,[26] while from 1954 to 2022, the ten-year Treasury bond rate averaged 5.56%.[27] As a result, stocks are more likely to outpace inflation over the long term, which can be an important consideration when it comes to retirement. At the same time, stocks have higher risk profiles when compared to some other asset classes. Market corrections and bear

---

[26] J.B. Maverick. Investopedia. May 24, 2023. "S&P 500 Average Return."
https://www.investopedia.com/ask/answers/042415/what-average-annual-return-sp-500.asp

[27] Aswath Damodaran. Musings on Markets. January 30, 2023. "Data Update 3 for 2023: Interest Rates and Bond Returns."
https://aswathdamodaran.substack.com/p/data-update-3-for-2023-interest-rates

markets are historically common, regular, and generally short term.[28] It is crucial to remember that investing is a long-term endeavor. The goal should be less about outperforming indexes and more about giving an investment uninterrupted time in the market—time to experience periods of rising prices and recover from periods of declining prices. The temptation to sell in down markets should be avoided.

One way to reduce the risks associated with stock investments is diversification. Stock investments can be diversified according to the size of the company, the style of stock purchased, and the sector in which the company operates. For example, stocks are often categorized as small cap, medium cap, or larger cap stocks, reflecting the overall size of the company and its market capitalization. Market capitalization is determined by multiplying the stock price by the number of outstanding shares of a company. Large cap stocks are thus usually more stable, but the tradeoff is they also generally have lower growth potential, while small cap stocks may be more volatile yet offer greater growth potential.

Purchasing varying amounts of stock from different-size companies allows investors, in theory, to enjoy greater stability and better growth potential with less risk at the end of the day due to diversification. The same concept of diversification can be applied to purchasing stock in companies belonging to different industries and sectors. Most often, different sectors are affected by different external factors, and this diversification strategy could reduce your risk and volatility.

Some stocks are considered growth stocks while others are considered value stocks. Growth stocks are ones which belong to companies presumed to be rapidly growing. An example of

---

[28] Yardeni Research, Inc. June 3, 2022. "Stock Market Briefing: S&P 500 Bull & Bear Market Tables." https://www.yardeni.com/pub/sp-500corrbeartables.pdf.

such a company would be Apple, Inc. with the release of a hot new iPhone. The item might be expensive, but to those who love the brand, it is worth every penny—you know the phones will sell out. Value stocks typically belong to older, more established companies that are selling at a discount to their true relative value. Procter & Gamble, a consumer products manufacturer with stock priced at $150 per share, could be seen as an example of a value stock.[29]

As you might expect, growth stocks can offer greater earnings potential in a shorter period of time, while at the same time being riskier. Value stocks, on the other hand, provide a more conservative and steady investment approach. One needs to be patient to realize a profit with value stocks, because the company represents quality at a discounted price. Diversifying your retirement portfolio with a combination of growth and value stocks could again offer some potential advantages. I typically suggest an equal allocation in both growth and value stocks since both categories rarely perform in tandem, and trying to guess which one will do better than the other is virtually impossible.

Stocks held in nonqualified taxable accounts are taxed as follows: Qualifying dividends are taxed at rates between 0% and 20%[30] , while most net capital gains in stock appreciation held more than a year are taxed from 0-15% for most individuals.[31] If a stock is sold after holding it for less than a year, the capital gains may be taxed at your regular income tax rate. In addition, brokerage fees for purchasing and selling

---

[29] Robin Hartill. The Motley Fool. April 19, 2023. "Investing in Value Stocks." https://www.fool.com/investing/stock-market/types-of-stocks/value-stocks/
[30] Greg Depersio. Investopedia. Sept. 11, 2022. "How Are Qualified and Ordinary Dividends Taxed?"
https://www.investopedia.com/articles/taxes/090116/how-are-qualified-and-nonqualified-dividends-taxed.asp#.
[31] IRS. Oct. 4, 2022. "Topic No. 409 Capital Gains and Losses." https://www.irs.gov/taxtopics/tc409.

stocks average $150 per transaction at a full-service brokerage.[32] Despite these disadvantages, the growth potential for stocks can still make stocks attractive in many instances. Because of their growth potential, stocks often outpace increases in inflation over time, making them a great long-term investment strategy.

Bond Investments

While stocks represent fractional ownership of the issuing company and a representative claim to a company's earnings, bonds are more like loans. Governments or companies issue bonds as a means to collect money for daily operations or special projects; bond purchasers, after a certain period of time known as the "maturity date," will receive the face value of that bond (typically $1,000), in addition to a periodic interest payment or coupon for as long as they own the bond. Assuming the company or government issuing the bond is stable, investing in bonds represents a reasonable alternative to stock investments, and in times of higher interest rates, bond investments might be preferable.

Like stocks, bonds can also increase or decrease in value over the course of time. Bond values characteristically move in the opposite direction of the overall interest rate. If the interest rate increases, bond values decline; this is known as "interest rate risk."[33] In turn, this fluctuation in value affects the total return you will receive on your bond investment. For example, a $1,000 bond (bought at par "$1,000") with a coupon of 7% interest would yield $70 annually until maturity. At maturity,

---

[32] Dan Moskowitz. Investopedia. August 17, 2022. "How Brokerage Fees Work." https://www.investopedia.com/articles/active-trading/022315/how-brokerage-fees-work.asp#:~:text=These%20fees%20are%20based%20on,full%2Dservice%20broker%20is%20%24150.

[33] James Chen. Investopedia. December 31, 2021. "Interest Rate Risk." https://www.investopedia.com/terms/i/interestraterisk.asp

assuming the company or government was still in business, you would receive $1,000 from the government or company. However, the bond could lose value if the market changed. For example, it could fall to $900 if interest rates climbed or the company or government entity had problems. While the interest income of $70 each year could still be received from the issuing company or governmental entity, you would lose $100 in principal if you decided to sell the bond before maturity when the market value dropped. If you had only held the bond for one-year, this transaction would only provide you with a total return of $970 in this scenario ($900 bond value plus $70 of annual interest). Similarly, bonds may increase in value with a decline in the interest rate, resulting in capital gains in bond value or growth of a company. Also, keep in mind that if the company went bankrupt and defaulted prior to maturity, you could lose your $1,000!

This is precisely why the U.S. government and municipal bonds are highly appealing: their default rates are exceptionally low.[34] Thus, while interest coupons are important, the risk of issuer default for a bond investment is of greater significance.

Similarly, bonds are also exposed to several other categories of risk that stocks do not have, such as:

Interest Rate Risk. Interest rates and bond prices move in opposite directions. If interest rates go down, bond prices go up. Similarly, when interest rates go down, the price of bonds can go up. The reason for this is when rates start to go down, investors try to lock in the highest rates they can for as long as they can. When they buy the limited supply of higher interest paying bonds, the demand drives up the price. Likewise, when

---

[34] Moody's Investor Service. April 21, 2022. "US municipal bond defaults and recoveries, 1970-2021." https://www.fidelity.com/bin-public/060_www_fidelity_com/documents/fixed-income/moodys-investors-service-data-report-us-municipal-bond.pdf

rates start to rise, people tend to sell their lower yielding bonds, which drives the price down.

Reinvestment Risk. This occurs when a bond matures and the investor is forced to look for new bonds in the market at that time. If rates have fallen while the bond holder was invested, at maturity they will be forced to either sit in cash and earn very little or buy the new bonds at the new lower rates. One way to minimize this risk is to pay attention to a callable bond's true maturity rate, also known as "yield to call." If the rate seems fair given the economic times, fair enough; if it is too low or you think rates may rise, stay away. In addition, you could ladder your bonds over differing dates to limit the chance that most of your bonds could be called at once.

Inflation Risk. When an investor buys a bond, they commit to receiving the stated rate of return for the duration of the bond, or at least for as long as it is held. If inflation increases, an investor's purchasing power erodes and could turn negative. For example, if an investor earns a rate of return of 2% from a bond and inflation grows to 4% after the bond is purchased, the investor's true rate of return is 2% because of the decrease in purchasing power.

Credit/Default Risk. When someone buys a bond from the issuer, they are buying a debt of that company or issuer. This money is repaid by the issuer over time with interest. For example, General Motors corporate bonds are issued by GM and backed by its ability to repay the borrower. U.S. government bonds are backed by the full faith and credit of the U.S. government. Investors should consider the possibility of default (non-repayment of your principal) into their investment decision. One way to look at this possibility is to look at a company's coverage ratio. In other words, how much revenue do they have on an annual basis to repay the obligation? Put another way, what is the cash flow in comparison to the debt service? Typically, the greater the ratio in cash flow to debt service, the safer the investment.

Rating downgrades. Ratings agencies, as explained below, may lower an issuer's ratings from AAA to D if they perceive the issuer is in trouble. If ratings decline, this can have an adverse effect on the bond's value.

Liquidity Risk. If an issuer runs into financial trouble or is not well known, the ability to sell a bond might be difficult. The market to sell the bond could be "thin"—in other words, there are not many interested buyers. This condition could drive the price down on a particular bond. If an investor were forced to sell prior to maturity (assuming the issuer was able to repay on maturity) the investor might find themselves with a loss on their principal after the sale was consummated.

When bonds are purchased at their actual value, you are stated to be purchasing the bond at par. However, you may also purchase a bond for an amount less than its actual value. For example, if you purchased a bond worth $1,000 for $970, this is called a discounted bond. On top of this, if the bond had an interest rate of 7%, your actual interest rate received on your investment would be slightly greater than 7% (since you only paid $970 for a $1,000 bond). Bonds can also be bought for amounts higher than their stated value. This is called paying a premium for your bond, i.e., paying $1,050 per bond.

Several types of bonds are available for purchase. A number of bonds are offered by the U.S. Treasury, including Treasury bills, Treasury notes, and Treasury bonds. These differ in their length of terms to maturity, with T-bills having the shortest maturity terms and Treasury bonds offering the longest. These differences in maturity terms influence the effect that varying interest rates have on the bond type. Bonds with longer-term maturities gain more in value when interest rates fall, but at the same time, they also have greater losses with increases in interest rates. Regardless, Treasury bonds offer the most stable form of bonds since they are backed by the full faith and credit of the U.S. government. In addition, U.S. bonds are typically exempt from state taxes; however, you still have to pay federal tax.

Investments in corporate bonds on the other hand typically carry higher risk in comparison to Treasury bonds, but typically pay higher interest rates. Corporate bonds are backed by a pledge from the issuing company to repay the "loan" and thus are generally safer than common stocks of a company in the event of bankruptcy or default. As a bondholder, you can think of yourself as a "creditor" the company owes money to. Depending on the seniority of the bonds you purchased, you may be near the top of the repayment list in the event of bankruptcy, or nearer to the bottom, but you will always be ahead of the shareholders of the company.

Bonds are often rated by private rating agencies, the three largest being Moody's, Standard & Poor's, and Fitch. They all utilize some variation of a letter grade rating, with AAA being the highest and most stable, but their specific conventions vary. On the following page is a table summarizing the ratings from the three most common rating agencies mentioned above.

Bonds can also be non-rated, which means that the issuer did not request (and pay) for a rating, or there was insufficient information to rate the bond.

The interest payments earned, as well as any value appreciation, in bonds over time are subject to taxation. The exception to this rule is municipal bond investments, since the interest gained over time from these bonds is tax exempt from federal and state taxes if you happen to live in the state that issued the bond. Capital gains in bond values remain taxable for municipal bonds, but you will not have to pay tax on the interest payments received. For example, say you paid $10,000 for ten X State municipal bonds on March 3, 2021. The bond had a maturity date of 2032 and paid a 5% coupon.

Moody's		S&P		Fitch		Rating description	
Long-term	Short-term	Long-term	Short-term	Long-term	Short-term		
Aaa		AAA		AAA		Prime	Investment-grade
Aa1	P-1	AA+	A-1+	AA+	F1+	High grade	
Aa2		AA		AA			
Aa3		AA−		AA−			
A1		A+	A-1	A+	F1	Upper medium grade	
A2		A		A			
A3	P-2	A−	A-2	A−	F2	Lower medium grade	
Baa1		BBB+		BBB+			
Baa2	P-3	BBB	A-3	BBB	F3		
Baa3		BBB−		BBB−			
Ba1		BB+		BB+		Non-investment grade speculative	Non-investment grade aka high-yield bonds aka junk bonds
Ba2		BB		BB			
Ba3		BB−	B	BB−	B		
B1		B+		B+		Highly speculative	
B2		B		B			
B3		B−		B−			
Caa1	Not prime	CCC+				Substantial risks	
Caa2		CCC	C	CCC	C	Extremely speculative	
Caa3		CCC−				Default imminent with little prospect for recovery	
		CC					
Ca		C					
C				DDD		In default	
		D	/		/		

Rates started to go down and the credit rating of the issuer went up. You sold an X State bond on March 28, 2023, for $10,595. You realized a long-term capital gain of $595.00. Examining these yield differences and your income-tax bracket can help you determine if municipal bonds are a worthwhile part of your retirement strategy. The taxable equivalent yield is an important concept when comparing municipal bonds to taxable bonds, such as those issued by companies or the federal government. For example, if you are in the highest tax bracket in California (39.6% federal plus 13.3% state for California = 52.9%) and you could earn 5% from your state municipal bond, you would need 9.54% from a taxable investment to beat that![35]

Combining bonds with stock investments can help you achieve a less volatile portfolio. Bonds pay regular interest payments, which can provide a steady retirement income stream, and they are considered one of the more secure liquid investments. However, bonds are not without risks. Changes in interest rates, political climate, taxation, and world events can positively or negatively affect bond values, and inflationary changes can undermine the benefits from total bond returns. Also, for corporate bonds, credit risks exist related to the company's value itself. Therefore, when considering bonds as part of your retirement plan, several aspects must be evaluated in determining whether to include bonds as an investment strategy and which bonds could offer you the best opportunity.

Mutual Funds and Exchange-Traded Funds (ETFs)

Mutual funds provide an additional topic of interest. Mutual funds are simply pools of money invested from thousands of individuals in a variety of different assets. For example, some

---

[35] Bankrate. "Tax Equivalent Yield Calculator."

mutual funds focus on an array of stock investments, while others may focus on bonds, real estate, or commodities. Many mutual funds pool investments in some or all of these categories. The obvious benefit from investing in mutual funds is their ability to provide immediate diversification amongst potentially thousands of positions without individually determining specific investments. Lastly, mutual fund investments could save you time personally since a portfolio manager commonly monitors and manages mutual funds.

For bonds, bond mutual funds also offer some specific advantages in comparison to single bond purchases. Bond mutual funds allow automatic reinvestment of dividends to purchase additional shares of the mutual fund, which is not something individual bonds can offer. Likewise, selling a share of a bond mutual fund could be much easier than selling a bond itself. At the same time, some additional risks are present with bond mutual funds. Since these mutual funds contain an array of bonds, a fixed maturity term does not exist, making payments less certain overall. Because these funds contain several bond types, interest payments and bond prices are constantly fluctuating. These factors should be weighed in making a decision about investments in bonds versus bond mutual funds.

Exchange-Traded Funds (ETFs)

Mutual funds have management fees, which can vary depending on many factors. These fees are disclosed in a document called a "prospectus." As you review this document, pay attention to the "expense ratio" of the particular investment. This figure is meant to show you the annual "cost" or "fee" you will pay to be involved in this investment. Fees detract from any gains your investments might make and require close analysis. A possible way to reduce overall management fees is to invest in exchange-traded funds (ETF). Unlike other mutual funds which invest in select stocks, bonds, and securities, an ETF invests in all the stocks within a specific market index. For example, a Standard & Poor's 500 index fund invests in all 500 companies included in the S&P 500 index.[36] Because the index defines where investments are made, portfolio managers are generally not needed to monitor and manage these mutual funds to the same extent. As a result, the management fees associated with index ETFs are typically less. Interestingly, because of these lower fees, index funds can often outperform actively managed mutual fund accounts. In addition, an exchange-traded fund trades like a stock and can be sold during market hours, whereas a mutual fund will price only at the end of the trading day even if you put the order in at the market open. As you consider stocks and bond investments for your retirement, the benefits of mutual and index funds may offer some attractive options. As always, the pros and cons must be assessed to determine which strategy is best for you and your retirement situation.

Investing in Annuities

Annuities, more than any other retirement investment option, are often misunderstood. I do not "hate annuities." Annuities are insurance products that can provide a steady income stream for your lifetime, even if you outlive the principal amount you invested. The guaranteed income stream for life is backed by the claims-paying ability of the insurance company that issues the policy. The money invested in an annuity is able to grow tax-deferred over a period of time during the accumulation phase; depending on the type of annuity selected, you then can receive monthly income for the rest of you and/or your spouse's life, called the distribution phase. However, different types of annuities have different

---

[36] Andrew Bloomenthal. Investopedia. April 14, 2022. "How to Invest in the S&P 500." https://www.investopedia.com/ask/answers/how-can-i-buy-sp-500-fund/

advantages and disadvantages, and understanding the nuances of each of these products is important in helping you determine if an annuity is the right retirement option for you.

Annuities come in three varieties, which are variable annuities, fixed immediate annuities, and fixed indexed annuities (FIAs). Variable annuities allow you to invest money into a subaccount, which typically looks like a mutual fund. Imagine a lollipop. The wrapper around the pop is the insurance company, providing the guarantee(s) for a fee, and the pop is a mutual fund—for example, the XYZ aggressive growth fund. The insurance wrapper protects the mutual fund at distribution and/or death by providing a death benefit that is usually your initial principal. Some variable annuities have income riders—additional wrappers—which provide protection of your principal plus some guaranteed percentage growth rate when you decide to begin taking income payments for life from your annuity. Like all annuities, growth of your investment is tax-deferred, including any earnings attained. Earnings are based on the performance of the subaccount's investment holdings. However, it is important to remember that once you begin to withdraw retirement income from the annuity, any earnings will be taxed according to your income tax rate at the time of withdrawal.

Benefits of variable annuities include the ability to select the different investment choices, or subaccounts, within the annuity. You typically have various choices of mutual funds to invest within the annuity, which may provide sufficient diversification. Unlike the fixed annuities and fixed index annuities, the growth of variable annuities is not generally capped and thus could provide greater growth potential. At the same time, there is a greater risk since earnings are linked to the performance of the subaccount itself, which will go up and down with the market. In addition to the possibility of investment losses, another major disadvantage of variable annuities is fees. Variable annuities typically have annual insurance company management and expense fees, rider fees, account minimum fees, distribution fees, and fund internal fees known as 12b-1s, which altogether can be as high as 3% or more per year.[37] In addition, some advisors will charge a management fee (commonly 1%) on top of the commission they received from the insurance company when they sold the product to the client. I call that double dipping, and I feel that practice—while not illegal—is immoral. Most people are unaware that the annuity paid a commission to the advisor because they do not see it come out of their initial investment and it is not often disclosed to the investor.

In contrast to variable annuities, fixed annuities are not subject to market volatility. A fixed annuity provides a guaranteed return of your principal under certain conditions. This guarantee, however, is based purely on the financial strength and claims-paying ability of the issuing insurance company. One type of fixed annuity is a fixed immediate annuity, where you can purchase an annuity in return for an immediate income revenue stream. For example, Jon is sixty-five, has $300,000 in his 401(k), and wants to create a paycheck each month since he is leaving work. Company A offers to pay Jon $1,600 per month for as long as he lives in exchange for the $300,000. The $300,000 invested in Company A's fixed immediate annuity is non-accessible, but a guaranteed income stream is provided for a period of time for Jon and/or his beneficiary.

The advantages to fixed immediate annuities are the low-risk, guaranteed nature of retirement income you will receive from your investment, as well as the ability to assign a beneficiary of the earnings throughout the guaranteed time period. However, because this guaranteed amount may fail to

---

[37] Dana Anspach. The Balance. November 26, 2021. "5 Variable Annuity Fees to Ask About." https://www.thebalancemoney.com/variable-annuity-fees-to-ask-about-2389027

keep up with inflation, a cost-of-living adjustment (COLA) feature should be considered with such an investment, if available. For example, if the $1,600 per month grew by 3% a year, in the second year Jon would have $19,776 of income, or $1,648 per month each year thereafter.

The third and perhaps most popular type of annuity is a new type of fixed annuity known as a fixed indexed annuity or FIA. Some call them hybrid annuities. Originally, the fixed annuity paid a stated interest rate and that was it. Today, the FIA offers the traditional fixed annuity bucket plus a market linked index bucket or buckets to choose from. When the insurance company receives a premium, a larger percentage of your money invested in an FIA is assigned to diversified bond portfolio of the insurance company, which has a steady and predictable rate of return over time. These investments have less risk than a traditional variable annuity since the insurance company guarantees the return of your principal for a period of time, which can be used as retirement income. At the same time, a smaller percentage of your deposit is invested in options linked to market indexes you and your advisor select annually. A market index "call" option profits when the market index increases in value, while a "put" option profits when the market index falls.

If profits are realized with the option included in your FIA, you enjoy a portion of those earnings, allowing your investment to have growth. Any profits are tax deferred. And if profits are not realized from these options, you still receive your guaranteed rate of return, the return of your principal after a stated period of time, and any profits you might have realized due to the high-water mark from your FIA. A high-water mark or point to point option is where your principal rises to a higher level than your original deposit over a stated period of time and then locks in to never decline in value. Because of these features, an FIA offers a good combination of upside potential with limited downside risk.

Think of FIAs as an insurance policy for your life's savings. If you owned a $1 million home free and clear without any lending institutions requiring you to purchase an insurance policy on the home, would you still purchase the policy? I would suspect so, because if there were ever a fire, you would ultimately lose a place to live without one. Therefore, why wouldn't you consider protecting your life's savings in the same way? FIAs provide such protection. In addition to tax-deferred growth and a favorable risk profile, FIAs also have many other attractive features. The commission earned by the insurance agent selling you the FIA is received directly from the insurance company and not from your initial investment or pocketbook. Likewise, FIAs typically have no annual management fees. The fees are based on paying a percentage of any gain realized in a particular period. If there was a negative return from the index, your principal and any gain you made up to that point would remain the same, and no fee would be paid that year. Think of it like an elevator. If you went up to the fifth floor and the next year, due to the market performing badly, the index went to the second floor, your account would still be on the fifth floor and start fresh in the new year. In addition, many FIAs offer enrollment bonuses, which can be as much as 5 to 10% of your investment. This is free money. Do you remember what our favorite investment opportunity is?

FIAs, like other annuities, might provide a lifetime income stream for you and/or your spouse if desired, and the insurance company protects not only your savings but also your investment gains from the index without the threat of loss. If you have an FIA which allows a beneficiary, these investment tools also avoid probate and facilitate disbursements to your beneficiaries more efficiently. However, it should be understood that FIAs are not "get rich quick" schemes. These are long-term investment strategies that should be considered with investment periods of five years or more. These products offer a great alternative to other fixed savings investments, such as certificates of deposits and savings accounts.

As a final consideration concerning annuities, many have potential fees related to early withdrawals in addition to possible commission costs and annual fees. Surrender charges are applied when amounts are withdrawn beyond a penalty-free limit. For most annuities, this limit is typically 10% of your total assets in the annuity per year.[38] This allowance may come in handy should unforeseen costs like long-term care or healthcare expenses occur.

However, surrender charges are highest during the first few years and then generally decline over the course of several years. For example, a surrender charge of 7% for excessive withdrawals the first year is not uncommon, but after seven years, withdrawals may not be subject to any surrender charge at all.[39] In addition, annuity withdrawals prior to age fifty-nine-and-a-half may well be subject to a 10% tax penalty. Understanding the fee structures of your annuity is especially important so you do not experience any unexpected surprises.

Making Sense of It All

Stocks, bonds, mutual funds, and annuities are all excellent options for retirement strategies, and each can provide sources of income during your later life.

Each of these options have advantages and disadvantages because growth potential, the ability to keep pace or outpace inflation, and overall risk vary among these products. In addition, fees and commissions combined with tax considerations influence the degree each may affect your

---

[38] Julia Kagan. Investopedia. August 10, 2021. "Surrender Fee." https://swww.investopedia.com/terms/s/surrenderfee.asp
[39] Investor.gov. "Surrender Charge." https://www.investor.gov/introduction-investing/investing-basics/glossary/surrender-charge

particular situation. While diversification efforts are an important primary strategy when considering retirement investment options, fees, taxes, and other costs must be recognized in seeking to make the best decisions. Asking numerous questions, doing your homework, and getting qualified advice from a professional who understands the financial, taxation, and legal landscape are important to help guide you through this process.

Expert advice is certainly important because tax codes constantly change. Legal statutes periodically affect strategy considerations. Educating yourself about various retirement savings options provides working knowledge that could help you identify sound advice. For the retirement products considered thus far, complexities concerning penalties, fees, and commissions can be overwhelming. In the next chapter, we will see how real estate investments can likewise be complex at times. The landscape concerning retirement investments is quite varied and certainly dynamic. Seeking both understanding and proper expert guidance provides a formula that often helps you navigate this terrain more effectively.

CHAPTER 4

Equity in the Ground

Owning real estate is generally a good idea. However, investors must realize that real estate markets are volatile, and real estate is an illiquid asset. The real estate crisis of 2008–2011 highlighted this fact. An array of opinions concerning the value of real estate investments exists in relation to retirement planning strategies. Many who were relying on a certain amount of equity and/or cash flow from investment property for retirement income suddenly saw their real estate's value evaporate before their eyes. Despite the collapse of the real estate market bubble, the fact remains that real estate investments and strategies can offer excellent sources of revenue and income during retirement. Therefore, understanding which real estate investment options and financial tools are available to you, as well as their benefits and risks, can help you develop a solid retirement plan.

In decades past, owning your own home was the norm. However, more recently, renting has become more affordable than owning a home (yes, even with rent prices through the roof). In 75% of the biggest fifty markets in America, renting was less expensive than buying a starter home.[40] This statistic can be viewed from different perspectives. From one standpoint, the failure to acquire equity in the home in which

---

[40] Leslie Cook. Money. July 21, 2022. "10 Cities Where Renting Is Much Cheaper Than Buying a Starter Home." https://money.com/cities-where-renting-cheaper-than-buying/

you live can be seen as a missed opportunity for wealth accumulation. With a rise in inflation and the growing preference of millennials to rent rather than own, the demand for rental properties has been steadily increasing in recent years. This trend is further supported by a 2022 Bankrate study, which reveals that real estate has become Americans' preferred long-term investment.[41] Moreover, individuals often find themselves grappling with the decision of when to pursue refinancing or remortgaging options for their home loans, as well as evaluating the potential benefits of a home equity line of credit. For older individuals, reverse mortgages could make sense, especially if there are not any beneficiaries to consider.

Understanding how to best use real estate investments and strategies as part of your retirement plan can be helpful in maximizing your retirement income potential. In this chapter, we will explore each of these areas in order to provide you with a better working knowledge of your real estate options. Whether you have numerous properties, currently rent your place of residence, or invest in real estate investment trusts (REITs), this information will assist you in developing a better long-term retirement plan. Hopefully, having this knowledge will let you sleep a little more peacefully in the place you call home.

Owning versus Renting

Determining whether to invest in home ownership can be a complex task. Several variables must be considered. For example, the duration you plan to stay in a home, or even in a specific city, affects this decision. Likewise, the specific location of the home must be weighed in relation to property appreciation or depreciation. Even your income may play a

---

[41] James Royal. Bankrate. June 20, 2023. "10 tips for buying rental property." https://www.bankrate.com/investing/buying-income-property/

role since tax benefits of home ownership may only be realized if a certain level of income exists.

Recently, trends among younger adults have shifted away from primary home ownership and toward leases and rentals.[42] Several reasons exist for this change. Compared to past decades, geographic mobility is much more common. Job relocations and a desire to experience different places in the world influence many to rent instead of buy. With shortened durations of residence, home ownership is less attractive. Not only are home purchases associated with mortgage fees, taxes, and insurance, but mortgage payments early in the term are predominantly applied to interest and not equity.

By choosing to rent instead of buy, money saved from avoiding some of these costs can be used as investments in other long-term opportunities. However, if you plan to reside in your home for many years, ownership often has many positive aspects. The main one, of course, is the ability to earn equity in the place you reside, thus allowing your living costs to provide some means of long-term savings.

Another advantage of owning your primary residence involves tax benefits. Interest paid on mortgages and equity lines of credit attached to your primary home are tax deductible (within certain limits), and therefore this portion of your home's payments allows for a reduction in your taxable income. However, it is important to remember this benefit is only realized if you have a large enough income to benefit from these reductions.

Additionally, property taxes and other items could be deductible from current income. Ideally, this money saved from a reduced tax burden should be allocated to other long-

---

[42] Joint Center for Housing Studies of Harvard University. 2022.
"America's Rental Housing 2022."
https://www.jchs.harvard.edu/sites/default/files/reports/files/Harvard_JCHS_Americas_Rental_Housing_2022.pdf

term retirement investments.[43] While home ownership certainly can provide advantages in acquiring long-term equity and reducing taxable income, these specific variables must be weighed when deciding which option is best for you.

With an increase in the number of renters compared to homeowners, purchasing rental properties also offers retirement income opportunities. Ideally, purchasing the right rental properties allows tenants to cover your costs of mortgage, insurance payments, taxes, and maintenance expenses while the property gradually appreciates over time. Assuming you began such an endeavor early enough, you could own the property free of any debt by the time retirement arrives. This provides you with a physical asset, and a significant portion of the continued rent received in your retirement years can be used as personal income.

On a smaller scale, you may choose to rent out a room or portion of your home, or on a larger spectrum, you may pursue an apartment or commercial building purchase. However, in any rental property situation, several pitfalls can exist. If your rental property is also not your primary residence, the income received from your tenants will likely be subject to income taxes. In addition, because it is a rental and not your primary residence, insurance rates are typically higher. Periods of non-occupancy as well as costly repairs and maintenance can also offset rental incomes and demand ongoing periodic cash investments. To top it off, depending on the cyclical nature of the real estate market and the varying appeal of specific locations, a valuable rental property could turn into a less-than-desirable one over time. It is important for you to get an education on risks associated with rentals prior to buying one. It is a good idea to have a conversation with an experienced

---

[43] Amy Fontinelle, Mike Cetera. Forbes Advisor. March 22, 2021. "10 Tax Benefits of Owning a Home."
https://www.forbes.com/advisor/mortgages/tax-benefits-of-owning-a-home/

real estate agent who has worked with many different rental property owners. Rental properties can serve as a valuable tool for additional retirement income. Seeking advice from a qualified financial advisor and an attorney can help you perform a cost-benefit analysis to see if pursuing rental property investments is worthwhile for your situation.

Reverse Mortgages

For many people, having equity in their homes upon reaching retirement is a given. However, they may not be interested in renting out portions of their homes, and options for accessing an equity line of credit are limited since they no longer have an income to support loan paybacks. In this situation, some consider a reverse mortgage a reasonable alternative, allowing them to not only access this equity through a type of loan but also avoid loan repayments. In addition, reverse mortgages are designed in most instances to allow retirees to stay in their homes in their later years while gaining tax-deferred retirement income from their home equity.

A reverse mortgage is available to individuals age sixty-two years and older who have adequate equity in their home to qualify for an equity-based loan. This federally sponsored mortgage, backed by the Federal Housing Authority (FHA), can be structured as a fixed- or adjustable-rate mortgage.[44] Fixed reverse mortgages can provide equity in a lump sum at closing while adjustable reverse mortgages offer an array of options. Some individuals choose the lump sum option to reduce their monthly expense burdens in retirement, paying off an existing mortgage on their home as well as other debts. Proceeds from adjustable mortgages can provide monthly income for a set

---

[44] Amy Fontinelle. Investopedia. June 10, 2022. "Reverse Mortgage Definition." https://www.investopedia.com/mortgage/reverse-mortgage/

term, an equity line of credit, or even a monthly income for life. As a result, these options offer an ongoing means to have money for expenses throughout retirement.

Reverse mortgages are not necessarily for everyone, and to be clear, these products are a type of mortgage loan which requires qualifications to be met and, eventually, balances to be paid. In terms of qualifications, reverse mortgage amounts and approvals primarily depend on three items: your home's value, your age, and the equity in your home. In terms of age, you must be sixty-two years of age or older. In addition, you must own your home. Loan amounts depend on the amount of equity in your home. Based on your home's appraised value and expected mortgage interest rates, reverse mortgages can provide amounts up to a maximum one-time amount of $970,800 as of January 1, 2022,[45] but no other mortgages or debts can be tied to your home. This requires any existing mortgages and liens on your home to be paid by the reverse mortgage proceeds first. While the maximum loan amount may fluctuate with your home's equity and mortgage interest rates, loan limits are generally around 60% of the equity in your home up to the maximum amount described if you are using the money to pay off your forward mortgage.[46]

The primary benefit of reverse mortgages is the ability to receive a portion of your home's equity through a mortgage product while you are alive, without having to pay a monthly mortgage payment to a bank. And all the while, you get to stay in your home! However, costs do exist. For example, home insurance payments, property taxes, routine repairs, and maintenance costs must still be paid by the borrower. Failure to do so can result in loan default and eviction from your residence. Likewise, reverse mortgages have administrative costs and fees similar to other mortgages. For example,

---

[45] Ibid.

[46] Ibid.

mortgage insurance premiums must be purchased, which typically costs 2% of the appraised value of your home. In some cases, this can be reduced to as low as 0.5% if the amount of funds received is significantly reduced.[47] Regardless, these expenses must be considered before pursuing a reverse mortgage.

The decision to take the proceeds of a reverse mortgage as a lump sum payment, as a line of credit, or as monthly installments of income can also be complex. Lump sum amounts are structured as a fixed-rate mortgage in which the balance that accrues each month is fixed and does not change. The other options are structured as adjustable-rate mortgages, where the balance owed each month can fluctuate based on interest rates. Many people choose to take the loan as a lump sum amount, allowing them to pay off other debts and reduce or eliminate their monthly expenses. Some may choose a line of credit in order to have access to funds for unexpected emergencies. The unused portion of your line of credit experiences growth, regardless of whether your home's value increases or not. This growth occurs at the same adjustable interest rate that applies to any borrowed funds.[48] While this does not reflect a sizable source of savings growth, it nonetheless could offer some benefits if you wish to have readily available funds for the unexpected.

Reverse mortgage proceeds can also be received in regular installments. The choice to receive monthly installments proceeds can be structured in two ways. First, a set term can be defined during which monthly installments are received.

---

[47] Amy Fontinelle. Investopedia. July 2, 2022. "5 Types of Private Mortgage Insurance (PMI)."
https://www.investopedia.com/mortgage/insurance/
[48] Amy Fontinelle. Investopedia. June 11, 2022. "How to Avoid Outliving Your Reverse Mortgage."
https://www.investopedia.com/mortgage/reverse-mortgage/how-avoid-outliving-your-reverse-mortgage/

The second option is the tenure payment plan, which features an adjustable interest rate and offers consistent monthly payments throughout your lifetime, as long as one of the borrowers continues to reside in the home as their primary residence. If the worry of depleting your reverse mortgage funds is a concern, the tenure plan is comparable to an annuity, providing a reliable income stream to help ensure you won't outlive your financial resources.[49] The amount received for each of these installments depends on the total reverse mortgage loan amount on your home and the age of the youngest borrower. For the right person or couple, each of these options may be an attractive way to receive additional income during retirement.

So, what happens with a reverse mortgage at the time of death? Once you—along with any co-borrowers or eligible non-borrowing spouse—have passed away, your reverse mortgage loan becomes due and payable. If the outstanding loan balance is lower than the appraised value of the home, your heirs have the option to utilize the sale proceeds to repay the loan and retain the surplus amount. However, if the loan balance exceeds the value of the home, your heirs can sell the property for a minimum of 95% of its current appraised value to settle the loan. The remaining balance of the loan is covered by the mortgage insurance that you (as the reverse mortgage borrower) have been contributing towards throughout the duration of the loan.[50]

To address concerns about the reverse mortgage potentially depleting the home equity that would have been passed down to heirs, some borrowers opt for an additional

---

[49] Ibid.

[50] Consumer Financial Protection Bureau. December 14, 2022. "With a reverse mortgage loan, can my heirs keep or sell my home after I die?" https://www.consumerfinance.gov/ask-cfpb/with-a-reverse-mortgage-loan-can-my-heirs-keep-or-sell-my-home-after-i-die-en-242/.

life insurance policy. This policy helps ensure that proceeds will be paid to the heirs, thereby offsetting the potential loss in home equity.

Before proceeding with a reverse mortgage, it is crucial to verify whether it includes a "non-recourse" clause. The majority of reverse mortgages incorporate this provision, which guarantees that neither you nor your estate can be held responsible for an amount exceeding the value of your home when the loan becomes due and the home is sold.[51] This makes reverse mortgages a reliable way to secure income in retirement without posing a risk to your other assets or inheritance gifts.

The lack of mortgage payments and the income received in retirement make reverse mortgages attractive for many individuals. Since the proceeds come from a loan based on your home's equity, the money received is nontaxable. Unfortunately, the proceeds from a reverse mortgage cannot be used to fund any type of insurance product, so long-term annuities and other types of insurance products used in retirement planning cannot be created using reverse mortgage proceeds. However, for individuals with equity in their homes who are looking to reduce monthly expenditures or receive additional retirement income, reverse mortgages may be a good option. Due to the complexity of these products, professional financial advice is certainly worth seeking out before pursuing this option in your retirement planning.

Mortgage-Backed Securities, REITs, and Other Real Estate Investment Options

Several real estate-based investments offer steady returns over time, and like stocks and mutual funds, they warrant some consideration. While the complexity of these

---

[51] Federal Trade Commission Consumer Advice. August 2022. "Reverse Mortgages." https://consumer.ftc.gov/articles/reverse-mortgages

investments is beyond the scope of this book, having some knowledge of these investment options might be worthwhile.

One common real estate investment option involves mortgage pools. Mortgage pools are essentially a group of mortgages which are packaged together to form a mortgage-backed security, or MBS. An MBS can be labeled as an agency or non-agency MBS, depending on whether it is backed by a government agency or by a private group, such as a bank, brokerage firm, or group of homebuilders. In essence, an MBS contains hundreds of mortgages within its pool, and investors in the MBS receive a claim on a portion of the principal and interest payments made on these mortgages by homeowners. The pool thus serves as a tool to provide risk diversification.

Common agency mortgage pools include Ginnie Mae (Government National Mortgage Association), Fannie Mae (Federal National Mortgage Association), and Freddie Mac (Federal Home Loan Mortgage Corporation). Of these, only Ginnie Mae is completely backed by the full faith and credit of the U.S. government, and only they provide a guaranteed timely payment of both interest and principal payments to an investor. In contrast, Freddie Mac and Fannie Mae are not fully backed by the U.S. government; however, they do have access to U.S. Treasury funds, making these also low-risk investment options.

An important aspect of MBS investments involves the nature of the mortgages pooled together. Early mortgages in a pool offer higher payments for investments, since early mortgage payments typically have higher interest revenues associated with these products. Over time as mortgages mature, the payments received decline as the principal owed and interest payments gradually fall. Therefore, MBS products can be categorized as either early or seasoned, and this affects the degree of risk and return an investor may experience. Because of this, choices in which mortgage pools to invest should be determined based on your individual needs, your age, and your tolerance of risk. MBS products with a greater percentage of early mortgages will carry greater payment potential but also have higher risk.

Benefits may also exist with private, non-agency mortgage pools provided by hard moneylenders. These investment products can potentially offer higher yields since some private lenders charge higher interest rates to homeowners. Though the mortgages are not guaranteed unless backed by Ginnie Mae or other federal agencies, the homeowner's insurance and the property itself do serve as collateral against these mortgages. In situations where larger numbers of homeowners default on private mortgage loans (as during the events of 2008), significant losses can occur. Therefore, you should be well aware of the risks involved when considering such MBS investments.

Real Estate Investment Trusts

Other investment considerations involving real estate are real estate investment trusts, or REITs. A REIT is similar to an MBS; however, these are much larger in size and can involve investments in properties as well as mortgages. Equity REITs are primarily property investments where revenues are usually derived from property rents or sales. Mortgage REITs involve loans to real estate owners, generating money from loan interests. REITs can be broken down into two distinct categories: those registered as publicly traded and those registered as non-traded. Registered publicly traded REITs are registered with the Securities and Exchange Commission (SEC), are usually traded during stock exchange trading hours, and are considered liquid. Registered non-traded REITs are also usually registered with the SEC but are illiquid and provide little opportunity to get out of them if you need your principal back. Both types of REITS usually provide higher yields annually since the investors take more risks. Also, the tax benefits of owning real estate discussed earlier are passed along to investors.

REITs can be offered privately or through public offerings. Typically, REITs may represent unit ownerships in shopping malls, office buildings, apartments, warehouses, hotels, or any combination of these. Instead of receiving a guarantee of mortgage principal and interest payments, REITs provide a proportion of ownership in unit investment trusts for investors. This, in part, allows the product to be more liquid. In many cases, REITs can offer investment advantages that can result in additional income for retirement. However, income received is taxed as ordinary income, and thus financial and retirement planning is important in determining if such investments are wise for you.

As you can see, real estate options for retirement planning are several. Some decisions may seem simple and straightforward, such as those involving whether to rent or purchase your primary residence. Yet even these decisions require certain variables to be weighed carefully in determining the best course of action. Other options are more complex and require greater knowledge and advice in deciphering whether they might be of long-term benefit. Acquiring rental properties and investing in real estate-based securities are examples of these possibilities. Other options, like reverse mortgages, could potentially benefit select individuals during retirement. Negotiating through this maze of retirement planning possibilities requires some degree of dedication to seeking the best answers for your unique circumstances.

As indicated in each of the preceding sections, such decisions are often complicated and can be influenced by a variety of factors. These include specific factors relevant to your situation as well as dynamic changes within the financial climate. It therefore remains important to seek proper guidance and to locate experts who can provide you with insights and details about each of these investment opportunities. History has shown that real estate investments often underperform stock investments as a whole over time, but real estate investments remain important tools to be considered in attaining greater retirement security. The key to success within this area thus depends on knowledge, understanding, and the proper expert advice.

CHAPTER 5

Avoiding the Tax Man

The single largest bite to come out of your nest could be taxes! Let's face it: Understanding taxes and tax strategies is a challenging task. This fact is obvious, considering that the current U.S. tax code contains thousands of pages![52]

Yet despite this volume of data, few (if any) modifications to the tax code are actually made each year, making it crucial to stay informed about changes and their potential impact on you. A notable illustration is the expiration of all individual tax provisions outlined in the 2017 Tax Cuts and Jobs Act (TCJA) by the end of 2025, which would result in significant tax increases amounting to trillions of dollars.[53] Just as your opportunities to invest constantly change as a result of laws, financial climates, and other regulations, so does our tax code. We all pay more than half of our income to an assortment of taxes: income tax, property tax, sales tax, and taxes on our gas, food, clothing, and internet purchases, to list a few. You get the point. Having a tax-efficient strategy is extremely important for your retirement planning success. After all, it is not what you make—it is what

---

[52] William McBride. Tax Foundation. April 18, 2023. "Testimony: The Costs and Complexity of the Federal Tax Code Demand Reform." https://taxfoundation.org/federal-tax-complexity-costs-reform/

[53] Howard Gleckman. Tax Policy Center. June 7, 2023. "Buckle Up. 2025 Promises To Be An Historic Year In Tax And Budget Policy." https://www.taxpolicycenter.org/taxvox/buckle-2025-promises-be-historic-year-tax-and-budget-policy#.

you keep that counts.

When tax strategies are mentioned, many people have the tendency to look at their past tax returns and assess the tax burdens already paid. While this is important, effective tax strategies for retirement look forward, not backward. Devising a plan to minimize your tax burden down the road can make the difference between experiencing your dream retirement and having to pinch pennies to make ends meet.

Because such evaluations can be complicated, seeking proper financial and tax advice is imperative. All too often, people fail to simply take the time to get the facts and the expert advice needed, and as a result, much of their life's savings goes to the government. Take a moment to reflect on the following illustrative example, presented solely for the purpose of demonstration and discussion. Let's consider an 8% gross return on your mutual fund, which is subject to ordinary income tax rates. After factoring in a 2% fee, the net return becomes 6%. If you reside in a high-tax state like California or New York, the combined federal and state income tax (50% for some individuals) would further reduce your return to a little over 3%.

With a net return of 3%, using the rule of seventy-two, it would take approximately twenty-four years to double your investment. While hard work throughout your life is commendable, it alone may not guarantee a successful retirement. Smart financial strategies, including a well-thought-out tax plan, play a crucial role in achieving your retirement goals.

The Tax Hierarchy of Retirement Income Opportunities

Let's review the preferred sources of retirement income options discussed earlier in the book. Based on both how retirement income is received and its taxable features, retirement income options can be classified into one of four categories. These categories, in the desirable order of preference, are free money, tax-free money, tax-deferred money, and taxable income. Nothing is better than free money, whether it is matching funds in your 401(k) or an inheritance received from a relative. I have even met a person who won a mega lottery! While this money may be taxed, you receive it free without any real effort. This option is always preferred, despite such opportunities being relatively uncommon. The first step in a tax-efficient strategy is to therefore seek to maximize free money opportunities whenever possible.

The next best option for retirement income comes from tax-free accounts. These accounts are not taxed, so you are allowed to receive 100% of these funds in retirement. Examples of such opportunities include Roth IRAs and Roth 401(k)s, municipal bonds, and loans from a fixed-indexed universal life insurance policy. Your decision to invest in these accounts can depend on rates of expected return, future income projections, and other variables. However, tax-free accounts are certainly worth strong consideration because of their avoidance of taxation. Consider the following example provided solely for illustration and discussion purposes, where we compare a municipal bond earning 5% to a stock investment earning 7% while factoring in state and federal taxes. Assuming a combined tax rate of 50%, if you invest $100,000 in the stock earning 7%, your annual return would be $7,000 before taxes. After applying the 50% tax rate, the amount you get to keep would be $3,500. On the other hand, if you opt for the municipal bond with a 5% return, the income is tax-free. In this scenario, with a $100,000 investment, you would keep the full $5,000 earned, making it a more favorable option than the stock investment, even with the 50% tax rate. By understanding these taxation differences, you can make wiser decisions about your future. Therefore, it is always important to consider the after-tax return of any investment! Tax-deferred accounts (the third best option) allow your money to grow without being taxed initially. Investing pre-tax dollars in these accounts permits a larger balance to compound, which in time results in larger growth. According to Albert Einstein, compound interest represents the eighth wonder of the world! Yet while larger growth is enjoyed, at some point the money must be withdrawn, whether during retirement or at the time of death. Upon withdrawal, these accounts are taxed typically at your retired income tax rate, which might be lower. Examples of these types of accounts include 401(k)s, IRAs, SEP accounts, and annuities.[54] Thus, while growth potential is favorable, taxation can make this option less favorable than tax-free accounts, especially if you are in a higher income tax bracket.

The last and least-favorable option involves taxable accounts. Taxable accounts require taxes to be paid on income from investments during the year in which the income was received. Income derived from individual accounts, trusts, money market funds, and others fall into this category of opportunities. Based on your combined annual income, you pay a specific tax rate on these investment incomes, which neither allows compounding growth nor tax avoidance. Such accounts may still be appealing due to a need for liquidity or immediate income, but their tax profile makes them the least appealing of the four categories.

When asked which type of investments offers the best option for a retirement portfolio, clients will often reply that tax-deferred accounts are the most preferred. But in actuality, free money and tax-free money usually offer better opportunities for maximizing retirement income. As with most tax issues, nuances and details exist which require proper education and advice. However, by using this basic taxation hierarchy to help you understand your retirement income

---

[54] Arthur Pinkasovitch. Investopedia. July 19, 2022. "Tax-Deferred vs. Tax-Exempt Retirement Accounts: What's the Difference?" https://www.investopedia.com/articles/taxes/11/tax-deferred-tax-exempt.asp

options, you will be more likely to ask the right questions and receive the best advice.

Tax Brackets and Rates of Return

In addition to the aforementioned tax strategies, a few other important pieces of information can help you better understand your unique financial position and taxation when it comes to retirement. The first item involves your specific income tax bracket. As mentioned, taxable accounts are typically taxed at your combined income tax rate, as are withdrawals from tax-deferred accounts. Therefore, how you structure your retirement portfolio and your strategy for retirement income withdrawal depends in part on your income tax rate percentage.

For someone with a larger income received during retirement, income withdrawals from tax-free accounts may make more sense in order to avoid high taxation rates. For someone with a lower retirement income, tax-deferred account withdrawals might be more tolerable since their personal income tax rate would be lower. However, in the case of most tax-deferred retirement accounts, individuals are required to withdraw a minimum amount annually, known as the Required Minimum Distribution (RMD), starting at age seventy-three for those born from 1951 to 1959, and at age seventy-five for those born in 1960 or later.[55] Therefore, one may have little choice if this represents the only source of retirement income. This demonstrates why planning ahead and having a tax-efficient strategy for your retirement is crucial.

In order to develop an effective tax strategy, you should be

---

[55] Bob Carlson. Forbes. February 15, 2023. "Key RMD Changes In The SECURE Act 2.0 You Should Know."
https://www.forbes.com/sites/bobcarlson/2023/02/15/key-rmd-changes-in-the-secure-act-20-you-should-know/?sh=1e1d06163846

aware of your actual tax bracket. Do you know if you are subject to alternative minimum tax, or AMT? If you do not know, then having a conversation with your accountant might be wise. The AMT is a minimum tax some individuals or couples have to pay when exceeding a certain threshold of income. This tax is in addition to your regular tax rate. This tax was designed to prevent very high-income individuals or couples from avoiding taxes through the use of deductions and loopholes. Many people are not subject to the AMT unless their income level reaches a certain amount, since the AMT was structured to apply only to higher-income individuals. For 2022, the AMT exemption threshold for individuals was $75,900, while the threshold for couples was $118,100.[56] Thus, incomes exceeding these amounts would likely subject you to the AMT.

For individuals in higher income brackets, avoiding unnecessary taxes on capital gains and dividends is similarly important. Capital gains from short-term assets (defined as those from assets held less than a year) are taxed at your ordinary income tax rate. However, capital gains from long-term assets (those held over one year) are taxed at a lower rate, as are qualified dividends. Long-term capital gains and qualified dividends are subject to tax rates of zero, 15, and 20 percent, which vary based on the investor's total taxable income. In contrast, the highest ordinary tax rate for 2023 stands at 37 percent.[57] As a result, it makes sense to structure these assets as long-term holdings whenever possible.

Once you have a sound knowledge of your tax bracket, you

---

[56] Tina Orem. NerdWallet. February 24, 2022. "Alternative Minimum Tax (AMT): Definition, How It Works, Who Pays in 2021-2022." https://www.nerdwallet.com/article/taxes/alternative-minimum-tax-amt

[57] Bob Haegele. Bankrate. July 17, 2023 "Capital gains vs. investment income: How they differ." https://www.bankrate.com/investing/capital-gains-vs-investment-income/

can better appreciate your real rates of return on your investments. Perhaps you have investments earning 8% interest annually. That sounds pretty good, right? But depending on whether these accounts are tax-free, tax-deferred, or taxable, your "real" rate of return can vary significantly. For example, 8% growth on a taxable account will be subject to federal and state income taxes, and if you are in a higher tax bracket, then your actual rate of return will be much less. For some individuals living in states with double-digit state income tax rates, nearly half their interest income will go toward taxes! Ouch. For these individuals, tax-free accounts could have much greater importance. As a general rule, the higher your tax bracket, the more valuable tax-free investments become.

Tax Strategies While Working in Retirement

What if you plan to work during your retirement? Perhaps, some consulting work or part-time employment sounds attractive to you. If this part-time income is simply an adjunct to retirement income withdrawals, understanding the potential tax ramifications of these activities is also important. For example, did you know that your Social Security benefits can be taxed once you reach a certain combined income threshold? If this occurs, these benefits will be taxed at your ordinary income tax rate. Part-time employment income contributes to your combined income amount and could trigger taxes on your Social Security benefits. Also, retirement income from tax-deferred accounts is considered part of your combined annual income. Therefore, if you plan on working, it might be in your best interest to avoid retirement income withdrawals from tax-deferred assets in favor of other retirement accounts. Consulting with your financial advisor and accountant is particularly important in gaining a clear understanding of such pitfalls.

Tax-Free Retirement Income Opportunities

Because tax-free opportunities for retirement income can be important for everyone, having a better understanding of these options can help you plan your retirement strategies. The first options considered under this category of investments are Roth IRA accounts. Unlike regular 401(k) and IRA accounts, qualified distributions from Roth accounts are not subject to taxation when funds are withdrawn in retirement. However, also unlike regular retirement accounts, Roth IRAs, and Roth 401(k)s are funded with after-tax dollars rather than pre-tax dollars. While this may not be ideal, many people's incomes rise over the years, leading to higher taxation rates. Therefore, paying lower taxes on income early in your life and funding a Roth account with this money may offer tax advantages in comparison to paying taxes upon withdrawal of traditional IRA and 401(k) accounts.

A second important source of tax-free retirement income can come from municipal bonds. Unlike interest gained from U.S. bonds, which is subject to federal income tax (but not state taxation), municipal bonds are exempt from federal taxes. Also, if you reside in the state in which the municipal bond belongs, then this interest is exempt from state income taxes as well. Because of this, placing some of your fixed-income assets into municipal bonds should be considered. The interest rate of such bonds must be weighed against other options of investment based on your real rate of return after taxes. Only then can you compare apples to apples and make an educated decision.

Of course, the ideal goal would be to have a safe investment option that offers high growth potential and allows tax-free retirement withdrawals. Stocks, bonds, mutual funds, and certificates of deposit cannot provide this since all are taxable at some point, and few can offer both safety and high growth. Tax-deferred retirement accounts are, of course, taxed, and forced withdrawals through RMDs are typically present as well. However, one investment tool does offer each of these desired features. Not only does it provide a safe, high-growth opportunity for your investment, but it also allows tax-free access to your money throughout your lifetime with virtually no limits on how much you can invest. This product is a fixed-indexed universal life (FIUL) insurance policy.

A FIUL policy is a retirement investment tool that offers both protection and growth features. As you pay your annual premium, a portion of that premium is set aside as cash, which is allowed to grow over time and accumulate wealth. Because the policy is tied to an external market index, it has growth potential yet also has a built-in annual floor, which ensures a minimum growth rate. That allows you to gain the growth potential of your money being linked to the market while also enjoying downside protection from negative index performance. FIUL accounts are one of the few options which offer both safety and solid growth potential.

By definition, FIUL accounts are life insurance products. Unlike other retirement accounts, FIULs allow individuals to create larger sources of retirement funds, which can later be accessed free from taxes in the form of loans. Ideally, you would establish a FIUL early in your retirement planning. A minimum amount must be invested into the FIUL policy each year as a premium payment based on the insurance company's requirements. Likewise, a maximum annual funding and loan limit exists with these accounts, which is established by the IRS. A violation of this code would be called a modified endowment contract and would subject the owner to tax on all the interest earned. Ouch! However, any gap between what you actually pay each year and the IRS maximum limit accumulates year to year. So, each year, your capacity to invest larger and larger amounts into the FIUL grows. This means that, over time, you can place massive amounts of cash into a FIUL without significant restrictions! This money is then available to you later as a tax-free loan against your policy that does not have to be repaid until you die. Even then, the loaned amount due is taken from the death benefit, of which the remainder goes to your heirs 100% income tax free! It should be noted, however, that these proceeds could be subject to federal estate taxes if the value of your entire estate exceeds the estate tax exemption amount, which is $12.92 million in 2023.[58]

For individuals who progressively increase their income over time and for those who accumulate larger incomes from business sales and other successes later in life, a FIUL policy offers a great way to place large sums of money in a retirement account that can provide tax-free income. In addition, because the policy offers a death benefit, you have the ability to pass along a specific death benefit to your heirs tax-free. The key is to plan ahead and establish a FIUL policy early enough so the large "bucket" for retirement investments can be created. While this product may not be right for everyone, a key component of this strategy is that you need some type of life insurance; those in higher tax brackets will certainly want to explore this tax-free retirement income opportunity.

While the strategies outlined in this chapter offer some general guidelines for avoiding taxes on your retirement savings, nothing can replace proper planning and guidance. As an example of this, the actor Philip Seymour Hoffman (who tragically passed away in 2014) had an estate worth roughly $35 million. Unfortunately, he was not married, despite having a long-term partner, and he had neglected to establish any type of trust for their three children. As a result, his estate undoubtedly resulted in a probate disaster with roughly half of his estate being lost to taxes.[59] The lack of planning and failure

---

[58] Rocky Mengle, Kiplinger. October 19, 2022. "Estate Tax Exemption Amount Goes Up for 2023."
https://www.kiplinger.com/taxes/601639/estate-tax-exemption-2022
[59] John M. Goralka. Kiplinger. July 26, 2017. "Philip Seymour Hoffman's $12 Million Estate Planning Mistake."
https://www.kiplinger.com/article/retirement/t021-c032-s014-philip-seymour-hoffman-s-estate-planning-mistake.html

to ask the right questions is all too common, and as a result, billions of earnings from individuals are lost to the government each year. Be sure you take the time to plan your retirement and reduce your exposure to unnecessary tax losses. Ignorance may be bliss in some instances, but when it comes to taxes and retirement, this is certainly not the case.

CHAPTER 6

Understanding the Social Security Puzzle

When considering various sources of retirement income, Social Security benefits represent one source often taken for granted. Many people falsely assume that when it comes to Social Security, no real financial planning is needed. A person works, pays taxes, and upon retirement receives Social Security income. What level of planning is needed? Actually, quite a bit! Did you know a retiring couple has hundreds of different choices regarding Social Security benefit options from which they can select? Choosing the best option requires a good understanding of the opportunities and consequences available. More importantly, failing to choose the right options could cost you tens of thousands of dollars in retirement income! Do I have your attention?

As mentioned many times in this book, an effective retirement plan involves several sources of income working together in harmony to help you achieve the best retirement possible. Diversification is the key. Many people fail to realize that building an effective retirement income plan requires careful consideration of how to most effectively file for Social Security benefits. For many, this consideration is the foundation upon which their retirement income plan is built in the first place. The variables when electing to file for your Social Security benefits, maximizing your monthly payments (perhaps with benefits to which your spouse may also be entitled), and avoiding or reducing potential Social Security income taxation are all important considerations when choosing your Social Security claiming age. If you fail to take into account how this decision may be affected by your other sources of retirement income, you may find yourself facing unintended consequences regarding your overall retirement income planning strategy. These ramifications on your Social Security income could include higher taxes, double taxation, lost growth opportunities, and more. For these reasons, a sound Social Security strategy deserves some investment of your time to be sure you are making the wisest decisions. This chapter provides a significant step in that direction.

Social Security Basics

Despite its conception as being a simple way to ensure retirement income for the majority of people, Social Security represents a rather complex entity. Confusion about many of its details exists. For instance, some presume Social Security benefits are only earned after a set number of years of employment. Others assume it guarantees a certain portion of their average income over their working years. Still, others question whether this source of retirement income will even exist when they are ready to retire.

Let's start by clarifying some of these common areas of confusion. First, you should understand who is eligible for Social Security benefits. In essence, the program works on an all-or-none basis. In order to qualify for Social Security benefits, you need to attain a total of forty credits, and these credits are earned through employment when you earn taxable income subject to Social Security taxes. An individual must earn $1,640 in 2023 to receive one Social Security work credit, or $6,560 to earn a maximum of four credits in one year.[60] Thus, most people who regularly work gain the forty credits within ten years. Additionally, even if you are unemployed for several years, you will not lose credits previously earned. Once earned, you retain those credits and can add to them at any time. However, if you fail to attain the necessary forty credits required, you will not qualify for Social Security benefits.

Secondly, Social Security retirement income only provides you with a portion of your income during retirement. Your replacement ratio, which is the percentage of your pre-retirement earned income that your actual Social Security benefit represents, can vary based on the level of your pre-retirement earnings and the amount of your Social Security benefit. Unfortunately, as your income level increases, the portion replaced by Social Security in retirement decreases. In a June 2022 analysis, Social Security actuaries conducted a study to calculate the replacement rate for hypothetical retirees across various income levels. The replacement rate represents the percentage of pre-retirement earnings individuals could expect to receive as Social Security benefits if they claimed them in 2023 at the age of sixty-six-and-a-half, which is the full retirement age for individuals born in 1957.

Here are the replacement rates they found:[61]

- For those with "very low" career earnings (an average of $15,006 per year), the replacement rate would be 75.3 percent.
- For individuals with "low" average earnings ($27,011

---

[60] Social Security Administration. "Social Security Credits." https://www.ssa.gov/benefits/retirement/planner/credits.html#:~:te xt=In%202022%2C%20you%20earn%20one,to%20be%20eligible%2 0for%20benefits.

[61] Michael Clingman, Kyle Burkhalter, Chris Chaplain. Social Security Administration. June 2022. "Replacement Rates For Hypothetical Retired Workers." https://www.ssa.gov/oact/NOTES/ran9/an2022-9.pdf

per year), the replacement rate would be 54.8 percent.
- Those with "medium" average earnings ($60,024 per year) would receive a replacement rate of 40.7 percent.
- Individuals with "high" average earnings ($96,039 per year) would have a replacement rate of 33.6 percent.
- For those with "maximum" average earnings ($147,775 per year), the replacement rate would be 26.7 percent.

This information is important for your retirement planning since you will need to make up greater portions of your income from other retirement sources as your level of income rises. Assuming Social Security will provide you with the same level of comfort you are used to during your working years can result in quite the shock in retirement unless you have planned accordingly.

Perhaps the most common comments I hear from clients pertain to a lack of trust in the government. Many speculate Social Security revenues will be completely depleted by the time they decide to retire. A little research shows this scenario to be unlikely. By going to the Social Security website (www.ssa.gov), you can access your Social Security statement anytime, and on that website, the Social Security trust fund depletion date is estimated. Based on revenues in the system, the Board of Trustees predicts when Social Security funds might be depleted by calculating several different variables. Currently, revenues in the system would allow 80% of benefits to be paid after 2033, which would decrease to 74% of accrued benefits to be paid through 2097![62] In addition, Congress has the power to alter several factors to further protect the Social Security system. Such interventions might include reductions in Social Security benefits received, changes to current taxation policies, and an

---

[62] Social Security Administration. March 2023. "Summary: Actuarial Status of the Social Security Trust Funds."
https://www.ssa.gov/policy/trust-funds-summary.html

increase to the definition of full retirement age. Based on this information, the chance that Social Security benefits will evaporate within your lifetime is highly improbable.

In total, more than 71 million people receive Social Security benefits. However, retired individuals and couples only make up about 87% of this figure. Disabled individuals and their dependents make up 13% of recipients, while 8.8% represent survivors of deceased retirees.[63] It defies logic that Congress would allow Social Security revenues to be depleted to the point each of these groups would lack income support, because we all need to eat. So, developing a strategic plan in managing your Social Security benefits remains a viable responsibility in order to optimize your retirement income.

Social Security and Taxes

You work all those years, pay income taxes, and even pay Social Security tax. You would naturally assume income received in retirement from Social Security would thus be exempt from further taxation. Unfortunately, this may not be the case. In some cases, individuals and couples must pay taxes on their income from tax-deferred accounts, as well as on portions of their Social Security income. By understanding how other sources of taxable income in retirement may affect Social Security benefits, specific strategies can be adopted to minimize or in some cases eliminate this burden. Due to the complexity of these issues, guidance from an accountant, tax expert, and/or financial advisor is often necessary. Unfortunately, many individuals fail to recognize this until it is too late.

The determination of Social Security income taxation is based on your combined adjusted gross income. This figure is a combination of your adjusted gross income, non-taxable

---

[63] Social Security Administration. July 2023. "Monthly Statistical Snapshot, June 2023."
https://www.ssa.gov/policy/docs/quickfacts/stat_snapshot/

interest income, and half of your Social Security benefits received that year.[64] Your adjusted gross income includes any regular or part-time employment income received, tax-deferred retirement account withdrawals such as 401(k)s or IRAs, capital gains, and taxable dividends. Depending on the total amount of your combined adjusted gross income, you may or may not be subject to having a portion of your Social Security income taxed.

Many accounting variables must be considered when determining your Social Security income tax exposure, but some rough parameters can be considered when examining your risk.[65] The following provides a rough guideline for how your Social Security income tax exposure is estimated:

For single individuals/heads of household
- If less than $25,000 combined gross income, Social Security income is not taxed
- If combined gross incomes between $25,000 and $34,000, a progressive amount of your Social Security income may be taxed (above the line on your 1040) ranging from 50% up to 85% of Social Security income receipts
- If greater than $34,000 combined gross income, as much as 85% of Social Security income may be taxed

For married couples filing jointly
- If less than $32,000 combined gross income, Social Security income is not taxed
- If combined gross incomes between $32,000 and $44,000, a progressive amount of your Social Security income may be taxed ranging from 50% up to 85% of

---

[64] AARP. April 26, 2022. "How is Social Security taxed?" https://www.aarp.org/retirement/social-security/questions-answers/how-is-ss-taxed/

[65] Social Security Administration. *Retirement Benefits*. Washington, D.C.: Social Security Administration, 2023 https://www.ssa.gov/pubs/EN-05-10035.pdf

Social Security income receipts
- If greater than $44,000 combined gross income, as much as 85% of Social Security income may be taxed[66]

As evident from the above figures, significant proportions of your Social Security benefits may be taxed if your annual income exceeds the parameters established. The formula above has been simplified and fails to factor in several other aspects of this tax determination. With proper expert counseling, you can minimize your Social Security tax burden in retirement as much as possible. Specific strategies for when to take Social Security benefits and when to access other retirement income sources become important as part of this effort.

The floor, or base amount, of $25,000 to $32,000 listed above represents the starting point at which some (50%) of your Social Security benefits become taxable. Once this floor is exceeded, the amount of Social Security income taxable gradually increases until it reaches the 85% maximum amount taxable at the ceilings. The ceilings, or maximum amounts, of $34,000 and $44,000 are referred to as "adjusted base amounts." Once these adjusted base amounts are exceeded, the amount of taxable Social Security income is the lesser of 85% of Social Security benefits received or a figure derived from complex calculations involving your benefits.

Based on these complexities, seeking advice from someone knowledgeable of your entire retirement income portfolio provides you with the best guidance overall in minimizing Social Security income taxes. The Social Security Administration estimates that 56% of Social Security recipients owe income taxes on these benefits.[67] Depending on the length of time over which Social Security benefits are taken, the difference between

---

[66] Ibid.
[67] AARP. April 26, 2022. "How is Social Security taxed?" https://www.aarp.org/retirement/social-security/questions-answers/how-is-ss-taxed/

paying taxes on this income and avoiding it altogether could be significant. Do you think these extra retirement savings might come in handy? If so, then developing a plan and strategy for when and how to access your Social Security income is a necessary step in seeking to maximize your retirement benefits overall.

Social Security and Retirement Income Strategies

Determining how best to strategize in relation to Social Security benefit withdrawals can be complicated and dependent on many variables. Therefore, providing specific guidance to your situation is beyond the scope of this chapter. However, a general overview can be provided to enable you to ask focused questions and better understand why certain strategies may be considered. Factors such as other retirement income sources, your income tax rate, your age, and your anticipated longevity all play a role in developing the best Social Security strategy.

With that, one of the first steps in approaching a Social Security strategy involves determining your full retirement age, or FRA. Your FRA represents the age at which you can receive your primary insurance amount from Social Security, and this age is based on your date of birth, since FRA has changed over time. For example, for someone born in 1938, their FRA is sixty-five years and two months. For someone born between 1943 and 1954, their FRA is sixty-six years. Currently, FRA increases incrementally to the age of sixty-seven years for individuals born in 1960 or later. Access to this information is easily obtained from the Social Security Administration's website.[68]

The reason knowledge of FRA is important stems from the fact that claiming Social Security prior to your FRA results in a

---

[68] Social Security Administration. *Retirement Benefits*. Washington, D.C.: Social Security Administration, 2023. https://www.ssa.gov/pubs/EN-05-10035.pdf

reduced level of benefits received. At the same time, delaying your claim past your FRA results in higher monthly benefit amounts. In fact, your benefits increase 8% per year for every year past your FRA; in some cases, this level of growth may be very attractive.[69] In addition, cost of living adjustments (COLA) are factored into these benefit determinations over time, often making delayed Social Security claiming similarly desirable for some.[70] Based on this information, you may assume delaying Social Security claiming is always preferred. This assumption, however, is not always the case.

For illustrative and discussion purposes only, let's examine the following scenario. A person born in 1950 has an FRA of sixty-six years. At that age, let's assume he would receive a full retirement benefit from Social Security of $2,000 per month (COLA, for the sake of simplicity, are not included in this example). If he chooses to begin receiving benefits at age sixty-two years, then this monthly amount will be reduced. Likewise, if he chooses to receive benefits starting at age sixty-four years, the monthly amount would still be less than his full retirement benefit but greater than the amount allowed at age sixty-two years. And at sixty-six years of age, he would receive his full retirement benefit. In comparing these three scenarios, by the time he reached the age of seventy, significant differences in the total amounts received from Social Security would be evident. At seventy years of age, the total amount received would be $96,000 if he had waited until age sixty-six, $124,776, if he began withdrawals at age sixty-four, and $144,000 if he began receiving benefits at age sixty-two. By delaying Social Security benefits until his FRA, he accumulated $48,000 less than he would have if he had chosen early withdrawal at age sixty-two!

In the above scenario, if the person's longevity was only to

---

[69] Ibid.
[70] Social Security Administration. "Cost-of-Living Adjustment (COLA) Information for 2023." https://www.ssa.gov/cola/

age seventy, then delaying Social Security benefits until FRA would have been less than desirable in terms of total retirement income. But what if he had lived until eighty? Or ninety? In these situations, the differences would have been reversed. At some point (which differs among individuals), a break-even point exists among early withdrawal, withdrawal at FRA, or delayed withdrawal options. If you knew your actual longevity, then the decision would be much easier. On the one hand, you want to ensure a comfortable retirement income throughout your life; on the other hand, you do not want to leave money on the table. Despite the lack of a crystal ball, making some estimation of longevity is important. On average, most people live beyond the break-even point. But individualized considerations involving health, genetics, and other factors must be taken into account.

From another perspective, delaying Social Security withdrawals past your FRA offers other advantages. Because your annual benefits increase by as much as 8% each year when claiming is delayed, your Social Security investment is actually growing at an attractive rate. In addition, with COLA, the ability of Social Security savings to fight inflationary pressures also exists. Because Social Security is backed by the U.S. government, investment risk is small. All of these features make delaying Social Security withdrawals potentially attractive, especially if other sources of retirement income exist or if early withdrawal results in Social Security taxation issues. In addition, spousal or survival benefits may be increased with delayed withdrawals even if you die prematurely.

Due to the number of variables involved in making these strategic determinations and the complicated nature of Social Security policies and laws, seeking advice from knowledgeable professionals is important. In order to formulate the best approach to Social Security retirement income, develop a plan early in accordance with your other retirement investments and tax exposures. Weigh the pros and cons of early versus later claiming of benefits. Make sure you have a solid understanding of all the nuances of the rules and regulations. With the proper guidance and a commitment to determine which strategy is best for you, you can avoid losing thousands of dollars. This could make the difference in being able to realize the retirement of your dreams.

Of all older U.S. adults, 97% could receive Social Security benefits at some point. For about 25% of these individuals, Social Security benefits comprise 90% or more of their retirement income.[71] Clearly this is not ideal, since individuals require 70 to 80% of their employed income on average in retirement to maintain their lifestyle standards, while Social Security awards a replacement ratio much less than this.[72] Therefore, a diversified retirement strategy is important, and with this, an individualized Social Security income plan is also essential. Failure to develop such strategies can result in unnecessary lost income due to taxation issues or from a failure to access your money when most needed. With a basic knowledge of Social Security benefits and the reasons supporting a Social Security strategy, you are now equipped to make wise decisions about your future with the assistance of a qualified expert. Remember, a sound retirement plan begins with a solid Social Security strategy as its foundation. Establishing such a strategy will help you better plan your entire retirement income portfolio and more likely realize a better retirement in the future.

---

[71] Center on Budget and Policy Priorities. April 17, 2023. "Policy Basics: Top Ten Facts about Social Security."
https://www.cbpp.org/research/social-security/top-ten-facts-about-social-security#:~:text=Almost%20all%20workers%20participate%20in,to%20Social%20Security%20Administration%20estimates.
[72] Social Security Administration. *Retirement Benefits*. Washington, D.C.: Social Security Administration, 2023. https://www.ssa.gov/pubs/EN-05-10035.pdf

CHAPTER 7

The Burden of Rising Healthcare Costs

Over the last few decades, healthcare costs within the U.S. have skyrocketed. Healthcare expenditures in the U.S. comprise over 19% of the gross domestic product, so it goes without saying that healthcare expenses in general are going to naturally affect your personal pocketbook.[73] For many people, these expenses have risen dramatically in the last couple of years. Household health spending has grown twice as fast as wages, and medical inflation has risen 1.5 times the rate of inflation over the first two decades this century, according to the Kaiser Family Foundation.[74] These statistics are worrisome for many Americans. For individuals in retirement—a time when healthcare needs often increase—these trends can be frightening.

Healthcare expenses can present one of the most significant financial challenges during retirement. The unexpected 14.5% increase in Medicare's Part B premium for 2022 came as a shock to many, raising concerns about the

---

[73] Michelle P. Scott. Investopedia. April 9, 2023. "Why U.S. Healthcare Spending Is Rising So Fast" https://www.investopedia.com/u-s-healthcare-spending-rising-fast-5186172
[74] Kristen Hwang, Ana B. Ibarra. CalMatters. July 15, 2022. "Health care costs keep rising. A new California agency aims to fix that" https://calmatters.org/health/2022/07/rising-health-care-costs/

overall burden of out-of-pocket healthcare costs for retirees. The Center for Retirement Research at Boston College reveals that median out-of-pocket medical expenses, including premiums, cost-sharing, and uncovered services (excluding long-term care), leave retirees with only 75% of their Social Security benefits available for other essential expenses.[75] Unless you have prepared for this rise in healthcare costs, you may well find your retirement income is being depleted more rapidly than expected.

Given increasing longevity, advancements in healthcare technologies, and a constant shift of healthcare burdens onto consumers, you can expect these trends in rising healthcare expenses to continue. Therefore, considering these needs as part of your retirement planning is important to reduce any unwanted surprises later in life. In this chapter, five ways in which you can pay for your long-term care (LTC) will be covered so you can best choose how to strategize and approach your healthcare during retirement. As a result, you will be more likely to avoid the depletion of your savings, reduce your potential tax burden, eliminate unnecessary costs, and still properly distribute your life's savings to your heirs.

Option 1: Medicare and Medicare Supplements

Different analyses predict differing amounts of how much a couple will need in retirement to cover healthcare costs. Research conducted by Fidelity cited a figure of $315,000 to cover cumulative healthcare costs for a couple at age sixty-five.[76] Given the staggering potential healthcare costs, addressing this issue becomes crucial when planning for

---

[75] Melissa McInerney. Center for Retirement Research at Boston College. August 2022 "How Much Does Health Spending Eat Away at Retirement Income?" https://crr.bc.edu/wp-content/uploads/2022/07/IB_22-12.pdf
[76] Fidelity. "Planning for Healthcare Costs in Retirement." https://institutional.fidelity.com/app/item/RD_13569_42402/retirement-planning-health-care-costs.html

your retirement. As an initial step concerning healthcare considerations, comprehending how Medicare plays a role in your overall coverage is important. Originally, Medicare eligibility used to parallel eligibility for Social Security, but this is no longer the case. As a result of legislative reforms during the 1980s, Medicare coverage and Social Security income do not necessarily have to begin at the same time. In regard to Medicare, one becomes eligible at age sixty-five, and if you are already receiving Social Security income at age sixty-five, you will automatically be enrolled in Medicare. If you are not receiving Social Security income at that time for whatever reason, you must actively sign up for Medicare to receive coverage. In fact, signing up for Medicare three months before your sixty-fifth birthday is recommended to avoid any mishaps.

What if you do not need Medicare health coverage at age sixty-five? Why not simply delay enrollment until the time it is needed? The most important reason is so you can avoid unnecessary costs. Failing to enroll upon turning sixty-five years of age may result in an expensive increase in your Medicare premiums when you do eventually sign up for Medicare. For every ten-month period after you are eligible for Medicare and did not enroll, Medicare Part B premiums increase by 10%. So if you delayed enrollment for five years, your Medicare premiums could escalate by 50% or more.[77] When you turn sixty-five, address your Medicare eligibility promptly.

Medicare is a federal health insurance program which principally finances acute medical care for the elderly and people with disabilities. With an emphasis on acute medical care, Medicare primarily covers hospital services (Part A) and

---

[77] Medicare.gov. "Avoid late enrollment penalties." https://www.medicare.gov/basics/costs/medicare-costs/avoid-penalties#:~:text=If%20you%20waited%202%20full,premium%20(%24 170.10%20in%202022).

physician services (Part B); however, limited coverage for nursing homes, home healthcare, and benefits are available. Medicare unfortunately pays few, if any, long-term care (LTC) services, and even Medicare supplemental, health, or disability insurance policies usually do not provide such services either.[78] Therefore, Medicare primarily offers benefits related to acute care needs but neglects to address the rising LTC needs in the country.

Let's look at some real examples (see chart below).[79] For the year 2023, when someone is admitted to a hospital, they pay an initial deductible of $1,600 for the first sixty inpatient days. For the sixty-first through the ninetieth day, they then pay $400 per day (25% of the deductible amount). After that, they could choose to pay $800 per day (50% of the deductible amount) for up to sixty "lifetime reserve" days or pay the full charge. For a specific inpatient admission, the "benefits period" ends sixty days after discharge from the hospital or skilled nursing facility. If another inpatient admission occurs after that, the aforementioned deductible and coinsurance process begins all over again.

---

[78] LongTermCare.gov. February 18, 2020. "What is Covered by Health & Disability Insurance?" https://acl.gov/ltc/costs-and-who-pays/what-is-covered

[79] Medicare.gov "Inpatient Hospital Care" https://www.medicare.gov/coverage/inpatient-hospital-care

When Deductible and/or Coinsurance Are Applicable for Medicare Part A

Inpatient Hospital First sixty days	Deductible applicable equal to national average cost per day
Inpatient Hospital Sixty-first through ninetieth day	Coinsurance per day always equal to 25% of inpatient hospital deductible
Inpatient Hospital Sixty lifetime reserve days (Nonrenewable)— Ninety-first through 150th day	Coinsurance always equal to 50% of inpatient hospital deductible
Skilled Nursing Facility (after three day in-hospital qualifying stay) Twenty-first through 100th day	Coinsurance always equal to 12.5% of inpatient hospital deductible

(CMS.gov, 2021)

NOTE: The monthly Part B premium that includes income-related adjustments for 2023 will range from $230.80 to $560.50 depending on the extent to which an individual's MAGI (modified adjusted gross income) exceeds $97,000 (or $194,000 for married couple). The Part B Deductible for 2023 is $233.

Regarding LTC under Medicare Part A, for skilled nursing facility benefits you pay nothing for the first twenty days if you qualify for these services. However, in 2023, for the next eighty days, you pay $200 per day and Medicare pays all remaining allowable charges. After 100 days of care in a skilled nursing facility, there is no additional Medicare coverage.[80] Based on

---

[80] Medicare.gov "Skilled Nursing Facility (SNF) Care."

these figures, it becomes evident that Medicare provides limited coverage of LTC needs. Home healthcare services and hospice services are covered for those who qualify, but the requirements are complex. Considering the potentially high healthcare and long-term care costs, it is evident that relying solely on Medicare will likely not be enough to meet your healthcare needs during retirement. Therefore, it is essential to explore and implement additional strategies to effectively manage these expenses.

Option 2: Self-Funding or Private Pay Using Personal Savings

Let's consider some facts about long-term healthcare after retirement. Among Americans turning sixty-five years of age, approximately 70% will require LTC at some point.[81] The average cost for LTC is currently approximately $297per day for a private room in a nursing home.[82] For individuals requiring LTC, the average number of years people use any form of services is three years. Of those who require nursing home care, the average length of stay is about one year.[83] Nursing home expenses can often exceed $95,000 annually as well.[84] These statistics highlight the importance of retirement planning in relation to healthcare needs, and likewise, many of these statistics are cited by insurance companies to encourage the purchase of their LTC insurance products.

---

https://www.medicare.gov/coverage/skilled-nursing-facility-snf-care
[81] LongTermCare.gov. February 18, 2020. "How Much Care Will You Need?" https://acl.gov/ltc/basic-needs/how-much-care-will-you-need
[82] Genworth. January 31, 2022. "Genworth Cost of Care Survey." https://pro.genworth.com/riiproweb/productinfo/pdf/131168.pdf
[83] LongTermCare.gov. February 18, 2020. "How Much Care Will You Need?" https://acl.gov/ltc/basic-needs/how-much-care-will-you-need
[84] Genworth. January 31, 2022. "Genworth Cost of Care Survey." https://pro.genworth.com/riiproweb/productinfo/pdf/131168.pdf

If you are among those who do need LTC later in life, such expenses can rapidly deplete your retirement savings. However, some individuals choose to establish a health savings account, or HSA. HSAs were established in 2004 and represent a way to save money for current or future health expenses while enjoying some tax benefits. In order to qualify for a HSA, you must have a qualified high-deductible health plan, not be enrolled in Medicare, and not be listed as someone else's dependent.[85] Often your health insurance company can assist you with creating a HSA, assuming your health plan qualifies; if they do not offer one, one can be established through any approved trustee, such as a bank or other insurance company. In addition, you personally own your HSA, so even if you change jobs or move to another state, you still own your HSA and can use it as you wish.

HSAs have some advantages from a tax perspective. First, contributions made to your HSA are tax-deductible, and you can choose how much to contribute each year up to a specific maximum amount. Secondly, the money in your HSA grows tax-free, allowing compound growth. In addition, some withdrawals are also tax-free if they are applied to qualified medical expenses. In general, funds from HSAs can be used to pay current medical deductibles, non-covered medical expenses, temporary insurance coverage during unemployment, LTC expenses, or other medical expenses. Some of these may not qualify as tax-free uses, but regardless, HSAs do have clear tax advantages, which you might find attractive if you qualify for such an account. Lastly, you can link your HSA bank account to a brokerage platform and virtually buy any stock, bond, mutual fund, and/or exchange-traded

---

[85] Jean Folger. Investopedia. October 30, 2022. "Health Savings Account (HSA) Rules and Limits."
https://www.investopedia.com/articles/personal-finance/082914/rules-having-health-savings-account-hsa.asp

fund with your HSA! See the potential? Hint! Hint!

Of course, some individuals in retirement simply utilize their personal savings and/or retirement income to pay for their LTC needs. This option is not ideal for most people, given the potential for LTC to be financially substantial. Regardless, some people are forced to utilize these sources to pay for their LTC, thus reducing the amount available for other retirement expenses and/or inheritance awards. Investigating other options is worth your while to ensure you plan properly for your LTC needs.

Option 3: Veterans Administration Benefits

Other options for covering LTC needs during retirement include government programs besides Medicare. Some people may qualify for veterans' benefits. For many veterans, covered healthcare services through Veterans Administration (VA) hospitals and outpatient facilities exist. In some cases, authorization for coverage of healthcare services at non-VA facilities may also be permitted when services are not conveniently located or offered through regional VA sites.[86] These veterans' benefits can certainly be helpful in reducing some of the routine costs associated with healthcare. In terms of LTC needs, veterans who are eligible for VA pensions may enjoy additional coverage.

Two additional types of payments may be received for LTC needs through veteran benefits for those who are eligible. The first payment type is provided for veterans who need healthcare workers to assist them with basic needs involving activities of daily living, prosthesis needs, and other aid services. Likewise, aid and attendance payments are also available for qualifying veterans who are bedridden, require

---

[86] U.S. Department of Veterans Affairs. October 12, 2022. "VA Aid and Attendance benefits and Housebound allowance."
https://www.va.gov/pension/aid-attendance-housebound/#:.

nursing home care due to mental and/or physical incapacitation, and have visual acuity of less than 5/200 bilaterally.[87] The second potential payment type is for qualified veterans who are in substantial confinement to their immediate premises due to permanent disabilities.[88] If either of these situations apply, additional VA aid and attendance payments can be received to pay for these services.

Aid and attendance benefits are available for any veteran who served ninety days or more in active duty, with at least one day in wartime, and who was honorably discharged, once they meet need qualifications. Widows and widowers of veterans are also eligible! As a result, tax-free monthly benefits can be received to cover LTC needs. For a veteran with a spouse, recent monthly amounts were $2,642 per month; for a single veteran, $2,229 per month; and for a surviving spouse, $1,432 per month.[89] Oh, and did I mention that this income was tax free? In order to meet qualifications for these aid and attendance benefits, eligible veterans and their spouses as described above must demonstrate a need for assistance in eating, bathing, dressing, toileting, and/or medication administration, and they must meet income and asset requirements.

Assets must be less than $138,489 in total, excluding one's home and vehicles.[90] It is also noteworthy that some veterans who do not initially qualify for pension funds due to an excessive income may do so after aid and attendance or homebound considerations are taken into account. Because these LTC need payments increase the pension amounts

---

[87] *Ibid.*

[88] *Ibid.*

[89] D. Rose. American Veterans Aid. December 29, 2021 "VA Aid & Attendance Benefit Rates for 2022." https://americanveteransaid.com/newblog/va-aid-and-attendance-benefit-rates-for-2022/

[90] Ibid.

received, the prior income amounts may no longer be excessive. I highly recommend you find a qualified attorney who works in this area to see if you, your spouse, parent, or loved one could be eligible. In addition to providing LTC income for aid and assistance at home, these VA benefits also help cover costs in skilled nursing facilities/nursing homes and assisted living facilities. Failing to inquire about these additional payments can result in leaving money on the table, so to speak. Because application processing often takes four to six months, initiating inquiries sooner rather than later is recommended.

Option 4: Long-Term Care (LTC) Insurance

LTC insurance, like any insurance policy, charges clients an annual premium in exchange for some degree of coverage related to LTC expenses. These expenses typically involve costs involving extended home care, assisted living facility care, or nursing home care; however, LTC insurance policies can vary greatly in their terms and features. LTC insurance policies vary in their timing of services, their scope of services, their availability of inflationary protections, and their duration of coverage. As an example, within most policies, there is an "elimination period" during which you are required to pay for long-term care services out of pocket for a specific duration—like thirty, sixty, or ninety days—before the insurer begins to reimburse you for any care.[91] The majority of long-term care policies available for purchase today do not provide full coverage for nursing facilities or home health agencies. Instead, each indemnity policy sets a daily benefit amount, which is the maximum dollar value payable per day based on

---

[91] Barbara Marquand. Nerdwallet. July 7, 2023 "Long-Term Care Insurance Explained."
https://www.nerdwallet.com/article/insurance/long-term-care-insurance

the type of care received. If the charges exceed the daily benefit amount, you will be responsible for covering the additional costs. Some indemnity policies cover provider charges up to the daily benefit amount.[92] Some companies even increase premiums after a period of time. Restrictions on which services are covered may exist or require specific physician orders.

For a male aged sixty-five, opting for $160 in daily benefits, three years of coverage, a ninety-day elimination period, and 3% compound inflation protection, the annual premiums can vary from $2,364 to $4,116 based on the insurance provider. On the other hand, females of the same age seeking similar coverage might encounter a premium range between $3,744 to $6,888, depending on the specific insurance carrier.[93,] which is significantly more than most home insurance premiums. Because of this and other variables, both the public and the insurance industry have seemingly lost interest in these traditional LTC insurance products. According to a 2020 Department of the Treasury report, sales of new long-term care policies reached their peak in the early 2000s but have been on a rapid decline in the approximately two decades that followed. Insurers have been exiting the market due to the product line's poor performance. Recent estimates suggest that fewer than one in thirty Americans and merely 7% of those over fifty possess a long-term care policy.[94]

---

[92] New York State Department of Financial Services. "Comparing LTC Policies."
https://www.dfs.ny.gov/consumers/health_insurance/long_term_care_insurance/comparing_policies
[93] Lindsay Frankel. Investopedia. April 17, 2023 "How Much Is Long-Term Care Insurance?" https://www.investopedia.com/how-much-is-long-term-care-insurance-7479941
[94] Justin Papp. Roll Call. April 27, 2022. "Lawmakers, regulators seek long-term care insurance solutions."
https://rollcall.com/2022/04/27/lawmakers-regulators-seek-long-term-care-insurance-solutions/

New alternatives for LTC insurance involve annuities with LTC benefits (or "riders") and life insurance policies with LTC riders. Both offer lump sum amounts, which can be used to a degree in LTC benefits. For example, annuities that offer a guaranteed growth potential allow a portion to be used for LTC, and any unused portion can then be assigned to one's heirs. Life insurance policies allow access to the face amount for the purpose of LTC needs, and the unused portion remains as the death benefit to a beneficiary. Each of these options have tax benefits in many instances, which may help one decide which option is preferable.

When considering an LTC insurance or annuity policy, several aspects must be considered within the policy. In some cases, LTC benefits may apply to skilled nursing facilities (also known as nursing homes) but fail to provide benefits for home healthcare, assisted living facilities, or residential care facilities. Based on personal experience, I have found a minority of people desire nursing home care, and thus these other benefits are quite important when considering an LTC policy. Other important questions involve whether the premium invested for the policy is available to your heirs upon death. The cost-of-living adjustment (COLA) rates of these policies are also worth exploring. Many offer a simple COLA rate at 3% per year, but a compounded COLA rate can be pursued, which may offer growth benefits despite the policy's higher premium costs.

Another important question concerning an LTC policy involves the number of activities of daily living (ADL) that must be impaired before the policy becomes effective. The core six ADLs include independently eating, dressing, bathing, toileting, transferring, and maintaining continence.

Most commonly, impairment of two of these ADLs triggers activation of an LTC policy, but each policy can vary. Also, each policy varies in terms of its elimination (or deductible) period.[95]

The elimination period is the period of time that must pass between when LTC needs are established and when an LTC policy offers coverage. Ideally, a policy should have an elimination period between twenty and forty-five days in order to gain the policy's benefits. As a general rule, policies with ninety-day elimination periods should be avoided.

In trying to determine if an LTC insurance policy is right for you, seeking expert financial advice is strongly encouraged. A major factor in selecting a LTC insurance policy pertains to the insurance company selling the product. When choosing an insurance company, it is essential to factor in the insurer's financial strength. Evaluating an insurer's financial condition involves extensive analysis and number-crunching. Fortunately, financial ratings firms have already performed much of this work, making it easier for consumers. There are five primary companies that publish financial ratings of insurance companies: Fitch Ratings, A.M. Best, Standard & Poor's, Moody's, and the Kroll Bond Rating Agency. Relying on these reputable sources can provide valuable insights into the stability and reliability of an insurance company.[96] In addition, state insurance offices can identify companies that have increased premiums on their LTC insurance policies over time. This alone should be a red flag. Researching the insurance company, in addition to dissecting the actual features of the policy, is necessary for making rational decisions. This, combined with professional advice and guidance, is

---

[95] Barbara Marquand. NerdWallet. July 7, 2023. "Long-Term Care Insurance Explained."
https://www.nerdwallet.com/article/insurance/long-term-care-insurance
[96] Marianne Bonner. The Balance. September 13, 2022. "Insurance Rating Companies Explained." https://www.thebalancemoney.com/insurance-company-ratings-462502

recommended when it comes to LTC insurance options.

Option 5: Medicaid

Medicaid represents another source of funding for LTC and healthcare needs. In fact, in California, as many as 62% of nursing home seniors are supported financially through Medicaid funds.[97] Medicaid is a joint federal and state health insurance program that is primarily regulated by the state, as long as they adhere to basic federal guidelines. Because of this, Medicaid eligibility and assistance varies greatly from state to state. However, individuals who qualify for Medicaid typically have low incomes and minimal assets. Once qualified, Medicaid may pay for an array of services, including doctor visits, hospitalizations, nursing home care, home healthcare services, and other LTC costs.[98] Regarding these aspects of Medicaid, three areas should be considered: the type of state Medicaid program, the determination of shared costs, and the methods Medicaid recovers funds.

Medicaid programs for LTC vary from state to state, with some being income states and some being assets/resource states. This distinction refers to the limits on either income or assets which are allowed in order for one to qualify for LTC services under Medicaid. California, for example, is an assets and resource state, and therefore specific assets may be either counted toward or exempt from these limits. Each year, the California Spousal Resource Allowance (CSRA) also changes to reflect inflationary and other economic changes.

For married couples, when Medicaid covers one spouse and not the other, a calculation of the share of cost for LTC services

---

[97] Susan Jaffe. California Healthline. June 10, 2022. "Medicaid Weighs Attaching Strings to Nursing Home Payments to Improve Care." https://californiahealthline.org/news/article/medicaid-nursing-home-payments-care-mandate/
[98] Medicaid.gov. "Benefits." https://www.medicaid.gov/medicaid/benefits/index.html

must be determined. Community spouses (also known as the "well spouse") can receive an income supplement from the confined spouse.

The third aspect concerning Medicaid and LTC services involves the recovery of monies spent by the state on the Medicaid beneficiary's behalf. After the death of a surviving spouse, the state may recover the amount paid by Medi-Cal from the deceased's estate. Monies spent for medical assistance by Medicaid provided since the fifty-fifth birthday of the deceased can be recouped from the estate after funeral and estate expenses are paid.

Though some assets may be exempt initially, ultimately all assets of the estate become vulnerable. Again, I highly recommend you seek the counsel of a qualified attorney who is skilled in Medicaid planning before you "jump in." You can find such attorneys through www.naela.org.[99]

When it comes to healthcare expenses in retirement, recent history supports that this will comprise a major drain of resources for the vast majority of individuals. Just as pensions and retirement plans have moved away from employers and towards individuals, the burden of healthcare expenses (including insurance coverage) will likely do the same in the future. Assuming Medicare, Medicaid, or other government programs will allow you to avoid depletion of your own retirement income can be a serious error in judgment. Therefore, planning an effective retirement strategy to cover these expenses is important.

In addition to the options listed in this chapter, other investment strategies and retirement income streams can serve to provide such strategies. For example, Roth IRAs and fixed indexed annuities might be considered for some individuals in planning for healthcare expenses later in life.

---

[99] National Academy of Elder Law Attorneys. "The National Academy of Elder Law Attorneys (NAELA)." https://www.naela.org//

Several alternatives exist, and decisions regarding which one is best for you require solid financial advice and a good understanding of the landscape. One thing is for certain: Healthcare costs are worth serious consideration as part of your retirement planning process, and seeking professional expert advice is strongly encouraged to help you develop the best strategy possible.

CHAPTER 8

Marriage, Money, and Retirement

Arguments and struggles over finances and money are common to married couples, and these issues spill over into thoughts, feelings, and opinions about retirement as well. In fact, disagreement over finances represent one of the most common reasons for failed marriages.[100] One spouse may live for the moment, ready to spend their savings or credit access whenever the opportunity arises, while the other may hold onto every last nickel in an effort to save as much as possible. When such polar opposites—or even less significant variations of these extremes—are married, dissension over money issues can develop, causing resentment and irritation. Because retirement planning requires couples to be on the same financial page, these struggles often affect how successful their retirement goals are achieved.

In a recent survey of 1,713 couples, 48% disagreed on their desired age of retirement. Over half disagreed on how much they needed to save for retirement. Likewise, 54% of couples state day-to-day financial decisions are made jointly, while 57% say that they make longer-term investing and planning

---

[100] James McWhinney. Investopedia. June 10, 2023. "Top 6 Marriage-Killing Money Issues."
https://www.investopedia.com/articles/pf/09/marriage-killing-money-issues.asp

decisions together.[101] Given these statistics, it is understandable that marital problems arise when retirement planning is considered. Fortunately, several simple strategies can help couples get on the same retirement page and maintain peace and harmony in their marriages through retirement. The following list of recommendations provides a guide for how to best achieve a retirement plan acceptable to both you and your spouse. As is the case with retirement planning in general, effective communication and advanced efforts to attain your mutually desirable retirement goals are foundationally important when making your individual and married retirement a success.

Discuss retirement lifestyle expectations. Married people often assume their spouses want the same out of retirement, and this assumption can result in a failure to have these important discussions. Does your spouse plan to work during retirement? Is there part-time work or specific hobbies they dream about pursuing in their retirement years? Do they expect to maintain the same lifestyle as before retirement? Do they want to travel or even relocate to another residence in their later years? Each of these are critical issues that need to be discussed and openly communicated for effective retirement planning to take place, and in the process, couples can better understand strategies needed today to make tomorrow possible.

Define your retirement target date. Do you know when you and/or your spouse want to retire? Perhaps your spouse desires an early retirement to pursue other aspirations, or maybe he or she enjoys his or her current career and wishes to

---

[101] Fidelity Investments. "2021 Couples & Money Study."
https://www.fidelity.com/bin-public/060_www_fidelity_com/documents/about-fidelity/Fidelity-Couples-and-Money-Fact-Sheet-2021.pdf

put off retirement to a later age. Setting a target date for retirement for both of you is important so expectations are in place and retirement planning aligns well with these targets. This likewise helps to reduce any surprises later, which might be a source of contention.

Assess retirement risks. Among married couples, as many as one-quarter fail to consider healthcare costs in retirement.[102] Healthcare expenses, along with other risks, can significantly affect the amount of income you will need during retirement and thus affect retirement planning. Other risks may include personal longevity, inflationary changes, investment conservatism, and aggressive retirement income withdrawals. Each of you individually and both of you collectively have risks that need to be considered when selecting a retirement plan strategy. Having both of you involved is important in selecting a plan that best manages these risks.

Work as a team. Two heads are better than one, but despite this, less than 25% of married couples actively participate in retirement planning together.[103] To create an effective retirement plan that meets your needs, you and your spouse should be routinely involved in these decisions. Couples who work together as a team to create their retirement strategies are happier and more optimistic about their future, and they also are less likely to be surprised by some unexpected turn of events.

Take an inventory and know the details. In addition to specifics about each other's retirement dreams, both spouses should be fully aware of their assets, retirement accounts,

---

102 *Ibid.*
103 *Ibid.*

healthcare providers, and other sources of income. Likewise, both should be involved in discussing estate plans and wills, as these can pose unexpected problems when poorly managed. For example, a husband with a sudden catastrophic illness may have failed to arrange a power of attorney agreement for his IRA or 401(k); as a result, his spouse will be unable to change the account. It is important for both spouses to take an inventory of all retirement accounts, assets, beneficiary determinations, and other account information. Meeting with an attorney to create wills, living wills, power of attorney documents, and estate plans can provide a much greater sense of peace when the unexpected occurs.

Know your number! According to a recent survey among adults, approximately 79% expected a comfortable lifestyle during retirement.[104] Defining what is comfortable varies from person to person and couple to couple, and therefore assigning a specific income number to your vision of retirement becomes important. By knowing your desired number, gaps in your saving structure can be better identified. Expected longevity, healthcare costs, and other expenses must be considered when determining your target figure. Only once you know your number can you assess whether your current retirement strategies as a couple will ensure the retirement both of you want.

Encourage each other to save. Regardless of you and your spouse's personality styles and tendencies toward saving, sharing a common goal can serve to encourage behaviors to make this a reality. Challenge one another to maximize investments in 401(k) and IRA accounts before leaving the work market. Make maximum contributions to a health

---

[104] *Ibid.*

savings account together. By constantly sharing and reinforcing your mutual retirement dreams, both of you will make a greater effort to save for that future. Everyone needs support, and motivating one another to save toward a common goal will likely strengthen both your retirement accounts and your marriage.

Learn together. Developing an effective retirement strategy can be complicated and confusing at times, even for the most knowledgeable of individuals. Seeking professional guidance and educating yourself about various options for future retirement income is naturally important. When only one spouse is involved in this process, problems can sometimes arise when expectations are not met, or opportunities are missed. Rather than assign these tasks to an individual, both spouses should learn about possible investment options together. Shared decision making is important, as is learning about all the potential opportunities available.

Have a plan! In my experience, I would guess only 5% of couples have an actual retirement plan—and even fewer developed a plan together that considered the expectations of both spouses. Without a retirement plan, the chance that you will enjoy the lifestyle you expect in retirement is significantly reduced. So, first and foremost, commit to developing a retirement plan together that considers your wishes for the future. This alone can serve to make sure you both are on the same page and may help reduce the number of money problems you may encounter moving forward. Additionally, it is critical that you reassess your plan at least once a year to make sure all your figures are up to date. I tell clients that devising a plan is a lot like flying an airplane from San Francisco to Hawaii—there are going to be lots of adjustments along the way depending on altitude, wind speed, weather, and more.

Other Marital Stresses Common to Retirement

In addition to traditional money matters associated with marriage and the challenges commonly facing couples in retirement planning, retirement can also present other difficulties for couples as they transition. After all, both spouses have established routines and schedules associated with their lives—routines that have become second nature. Suddenly developing new routines or adjusting to a spouse's new schedule can trigger stress and frustration on occasion. Perhaps the time spent together becomes significantly increased in a way neither person is prepared for, or changes in how they relate to one another occur as both are more involved in one another's lives.

Like many other life transitions, retirement is often associated with an initial "honeymoon" period. Beginning this new period of one's life is often filled with anticipation and excitement. After a length of time, that can be followed by a period of disenchantment as reality sets in and expectations are perhaps not met. Maybe the lifestyle you wished for is impossible due to financial or other barriers, or the activities and experiences you thought would be fulfilling fail to satisfy your needs. Keeping this period of disenchantment (if it occurs) to a minimum is important since this can develop into overt depression. One of the ways this can be accomplished is through a degree of psychological preparation beforehand.

Sharing information and communicating with your spouse before retirement can help enable you to make the transition more easily. Actively expressing your hopes for retirement and a willingness to compromise are key factors in making successful adjustments. For example, both of you may have expressed a desire to travel in retirement, but travel for one may mean touring the country in a recreational vehicle, while travel to the other means exotic trips to Europe. Knowing this ahead of time and working out some compromises can alleviate stress and help facilitate the retirement transition.

Often, couples will make plans to relocate in retirement to an area they thought they would like. Yet in some instances, the new location lacks friends and the familiar activities they previously enjoyed. This can add to difficulties in retirement, which may be completely unexpected. Therefore, if relocation is in your plans, renting a home for a period of time to try it out may be in your best interest. If this can be done before retirement, all the better. Another strategy couples often consider is that of parallel play. Parallel play allows each spouse to have time and space for their own specific activities even if the other spouse does not share the same level of interest. This strategy may help ease the transition by ensuring both spouses still have personal time alone without being overwhelmed by an increased amount of the couple's time.

Whether it pertains to financial matters or psychological factors, investing time into your retirement dreams in advance can help make the transition more pleasurable and less stressful. Mutual participation and retirement planning help spouses better appreciate one another's wishes for the future while potentially reducing gaps in savings. Open dialogue combined with a willingness to compromise can go a long way in making sure expectations are realistic. Both financial matters and retirement can pose challenges for marriages, but by being proactive, these challenges can be anticipated and better managed in time.

CHAPTER 9

Estate Planning

Imagine you have worked all your life and saved diligently for your retirement. Due to your efforts as well as some good fortune, you have amassed a sizable estate. Life is good. However, amidst your hectic schedule and numerous responsibilities, planning how your estate will be managed and distributed after your death fell to the bottom on your list of priorities.

And honestly, the thought of determining who would inherit your assets upon your demise seemed rather morbid and depressing. So, you decided to delay such planning until later in life, when such issues might be more relevant.

Now, suppose you experienced some unfortunate accident or illness that left you incapacitated and unable to make such decisions about your estate, or imagine a scenario where you unexpectedly experience a massive heart attack and pass away. What would happen to your wealth and assets?

Failing to have a proper plan in place for your estate could result in significant and costly consequences for your loved ones. Fortunately, even a modest amount of estate planning can empower couples to minimize—or even eliminate—federal and state estate taxes, as well as state inheritance taxes.

Additionally, there are strategies to reduce the income tax burden on beneficiaries. Without such a plan, the tax liabilities your heirs might face could be substantial.[105] Unfortunately, such occurrences happen all too frequently. Amy Winehouse, Bob Marley, Barry White, and Jimi Hendrix are among some of the more notable celebrities who have passed away without proper estate planning, resulting in substantial tax ramifications to their residual estates.

Though you may at first assume estate planning is only for those with large amounts of assets, this assumption is far from accurate. Estate planning goes well beyond taxation avoidance. Being able to control how your affairs are handled and who will receive your assets upon your death is important for almost everyone. Taking the time to be responsible now prevents your relatives from having to struggle later through many of the complexities of probate and estate administration. In this chapter, you will gain an appreciation of the benefits of estate planning so you can begin to consider this important aspect of retirement planning.

An Overview of Estate Planning

For many people, estate planning is perceived as simply a means of determining how their assets will be distributed upon their death. Certainly, this function is a major part of estate planning. However, several components are involved in this process, in addition to asset distribution. For example, estate planning involves strategies to avoid or minimize tax exposure of your assets after death so maximum amounts of wealth can be transferred to your heirs. Likewise, estate planning also involves the determination of who can make decisions for you in the event you become incapacitated. These issues can be particularly important not only in the

---

[105] Donna Fuscaldo. Investopedia. May 30, 2021 "4 Reasons Estate Planning Is So Important."
https://www.investopedia.com/articles/wealth-management/122915/4-reasons-estate-planning-so-important.asp

management of your assets and properties but also in the management of your health and medical decisions.

The basic components of estate planning involve the creation of a last will and testament, determination of a power of attorney, establishment of a living will, and assignment of a healthcare proxy. In addition, creating a living trust may be necessary as part of your estate planning. Each of these components should be explored when planning your estate so your wishes are honored in the event you are unable to communicate them to others verbally and/or with a sound mind. The repercussions of failing to plan can result in many avoidable negative consequences.

As a general rule, several steps should be taken as part of estate planning. First, you should take an inventory of your personal assets and properties to appreciate items and issues to address at least annually. Secondly, you should devise a plan for how you wish these assets to be handled. In other words, who or what entity should inherit these assets upon your death, and when? Next, often one of the most challenging considerations you need to determine is who is capable of handling your personal, business, and medical affairs if you cannot do so. Identifying someone who is trustworthy and also willing to take on these responsibilities ahead of time is important. Once these tasks have been completed, you are then prepared to create the necessary documents in your estate planning with professional guidance.

Because state and federal estate law is constantly changing, assistance from experts in your estate planning efforts is essential. While financial advisors can provide useful information in many cases, attorneys proficient in tax law, probate law, and estate planning offer welcome assistance in determining how best to achieve your goals. Proper legal professionals can address issues regarding tax exemption limits on gifts and inheritances, benefits of various trusts, and structuring current assets to avoid taxation. Once such advice is received, you can then establish the necessary components of your estate to meet your unique objectives.

Wills and Probate

A last will and testament essentially fulfills three essential functions. One is to express how your assets will be distributed after your death, and a second is to name the executor of your estate. A third function of your will is to assign guardianship of any dependent children you may have. Regardless of your total net worth, establishing a will is important. Even if your estate is small, failing to have a will can result in ambiguity for your loved ones in knowing your wishes; from a more practical standpoint, this situation can create greater complexities for them in managing your estate after you are gone.

An important part of your will is to name your estate's executor. Upon your death, the executor of your estate will petition the court to initiate the process of probate. Probate is simply the court-supervised process of transferring a deceased person's assets to their heirs and beneficiaries as outlined in a will, or in the case a will is not present, as outlined by legal statutes. Upon receiving the petition from your executor, the court officially appoints the executor as the one in charge of your estate. This then requires the executor to distribute properties and assets as outlined by your will, process all claims from creditors against your estate, and file necessary tax returns for your estate. If an executor is not named in your will or a will does not exist, any family member or interested party may petition the court to begin the probate process. In this instance, the court will then assign an administrator to perform these same functions.

When a will does not exist, one's estate is said to be "intestate." As a result, you have no say in how your assets will be distributed, and typically the probate process determines where your assets go based on individual state legislation regarding inheritance laws. In addition to being unable to guide these distributions as you might have wished, intestate situations typically expose your assets to greater taxation. Instead of being able to allocate your assets to a spouse or to various trusts that may enjoy tax exemptions, gross assets (after debts are paid and administrative expenses considered) are vulnerable to high estate taxation. This can result in tremendous losses in asset value if one's estate is substantially large.

The process of probate can also be both expensive and time consuming, and the lack of a will can extend these costs and durations significantly. In fact, legal and other fees associated with probate can easily run in the thousands of dollars, and often the process can extend well beyond a year. Effective estate planning can reduce these factors substantially in many cases. In some circumstances, the process of probate can be completely avoided through effective estate planning. Planning properly enough to allow your family to avoid such unpleasant proceedings is certainly worthwhile and could result in preserving more of your assets for their benefit as a result.

A noteworthy exception to a will's power to distribute assets according to your wishes involves beneficiary determinations on specific accounts. Insurance policies, annuities, pay-on-death accounts, transfer-on-death accounts, and qualified and non-qualified retirement plans and accounts all have beneficiary determinations where a direct transfer of assets occurs to beneficiaries. Regardless of what distribution guidelines may exist within a will, these beneficiary determinations take precedence. This issue can be significant if a former spouse was originally listed on such an account or policy and the beneficiary designation was never revised after the separation. Regardless of current situations, the former spouse would receive those assets even if one's will stated otherwise.

As a general rule, you should review your will as well as your beneficiary designations on various policies and accounts annually. In addition, major changes in your financial situation or in your life should similarly prompt reassessment of these estate-planning documents. In this way, you can be more certain your wishes will be honored, and you preserve as much of your assets for your heirs as possible.

Advanced Healthcare Directives and Power of Attorney

In addition to your will and testament, estate planning also involves considerations concerning who should manage your affairs in the event that you cannot. Such affairs may involve important health- care and medical decisions while others may involve your finances or your business. Advanced healthcare directives and power of attorney designations address these situations and are integral parts of estate planning. Imagine being kept on artificial life support against your wishes as your estate's assets decline to help pay for your care, or imagine a failing business resulting from your incapacitation and a lack of proper leadership. These scenarios depict the importance of these two areas of estate planning.

Advanced healthcare directives involve two main considerations. One consideration is that of a living will and the other is the determination of a healthcare proxy or surrogate. A living will is simply a document that states your preferences regarding specific aspects of medical care you wish to have imposed or not imposed on you in the event of a catastrophic illness or injury. Such a document may indicate your preferences about assisted living care, nursing home care, home care, artificial life support, the use of intravenous fluids, artificial measures of nutrition, and more. These determinations allow your wishes to be known by your family as well as by healthcare personnel, so the stress, anxiety, and debate about such decisions can be avoided and your wishes honored. Notably, such decisions require personal contemplation about many factors.

Determination of a healthcare surrogate is somewhat different. Since a living will cannot anticipate each and every medical circumstance, assigning an individual to make medical decisions for you is important in the event that you are unable to make them. The person you choose as your healthcare surrogate ideally should understand and appreciate your perspectives on health and the typical choices you would make, since they are acting on your behalf. In other words, their decisions are not based on their personal choices, but on their interpretation of what you would have chosen to do, given the circumstances. Again, making this part of your estate planning is important in achieving the goals you desire.

While not related to health and medical affairs, the assignment of a power of attorney to an individual is somewhat similar to the appointment of a health surrogate. However, a power of attorney designation awards another person the right and authority to act on your behalf in other affairs, in the event you become incapacitated. Power of attorney designations can apply only to specific circumstances, or they may be more general in nature. For example, you may award someone the power to pay your bills, sign contracts on your behalf, or even withdraw money from your accounts. A power of attorney designation does not permit the agent to take any of your assets unless this has been expressly stated. The importance of power of attorney is to ensure your wishes are continued even when you are no longer able to accurately express them or perform them. Like the executor of your will and your healthcare surrogate, choosing someone capable and trustworthy to handle these tasks at hand is important. Another matter to consider is making your POA a "springing power," wherein the agent springs into power when you become incapacitated, or wherein the agent has the authority to act in your stead immediately the date the document is signed.

Tax Considerations and Trusts

Among the many advantages estate planning offers, tax-reducing strategies represent one of the more significant ones. Simply by establishing a will, any assets left to a spouse or to a charitable organization are generally tax-exempt on the federal level without any limitations.[106] Assets left to anyone else, however, have limitations to their tax-exempt status. As of 2023, up to $12.92 million in assets may be awarded to non-spouse individuals without being taxed; however, this figure also includes any values received from real estate, life insurance, retirement assets, investments, and more.[107] This figure changes annually, and ongoing knowledge of legislative changes is necessary to be sure your estate plans are current.

For individuals with larger estates, creative estate planning is needed to avoid unnecessary taxes if these limits are likely to be exceeded. It's worth noting that the Tax Cuts and Jobs Act (TCJA) doubled the exemption amount to $11.18 million in 2018, indexing to inflation.

However, this provision is set to expire on January 1, 2026, resulting in a return to the previous exemption amount of $5 million (adjusted for inflation) as of 2017.[108]

Several examples can be provided for how estate planning might help avoid the tax exposure of your assets at death.

---

[106] Kay Bell. Nerdwallet. May 17, 2023. "Estate Tax: Definition, Tax Rates and Who Pays in 2023."
https://www.nerdwallet.com/article/taxes/estate-tax
[107] Ibid.
[108] Jim Probasco. Investopedia. February 16, 2023. "Estate Tax Exemption: How Much It Is and How to Calculate It."
https://www.investopedia.com/estate-tax-exemption-2021-definition-5114715

One example is that up to \$17,000 per year can be given to any single individual without being taxed.[109] Likewise, payments for a relative's college tuition can be made without gift tax.[110]

Payment for medical expenses may also qualify and be tax exempt.[111] Options exist, such as these, which may allow you to fall within tax-exempt ranges of inheritances left to your family and other entities, and estate planning in advance should be pursued to optimize these opportunities. Establishing a trust is another possible strategy which may reduce your tax exposure, in addition to allowing you to better define how your assets will be distributed upon your death. Trusts are generally categorized as either living trusts, which are established during one's lifetime, or testamentary trusts, which are typically established in a will at the time of death. Living trusts can be further characterized as either revocable or irrevocable trusts. Revocable trusts simply imply you retain control of the assets in the trust while living. In contrast, you cannot alter or change irrevocable trusts (including beneficiaries of the trust) once established *without the consent of the existing beneficiary.* In addition, once property is transferred to an irrevocable trust, you (as the grantor) typically lose all control of the asset.

Unlike wills, which deal with assets in a general fashion, trusts identify how specific assets will be handled, and several different types of trusts exist. For example, a credit shelter trust (also known as a bypass trust or family trust) allows you to

---

[109] Ibid.

[110] Jean Folger. Investopedia. March 1, 2023. "Tax-Smart Ways to Help Your Kids or Grandkids Pay for College." https://www.investopedia.com/articles/personal-finance/012114/taxsmart-ways-help-your-kidsgrandkids-pay-college.asp

[111] Julie Garber. The Balance. November 7, 2022. "What Gifts Are Not Subject to the Gift Tax?" https://www.thebalancemoney.com/what-gifts-are-not-subject-to-the-gift-tax-3505684

place any amount of assets within the trust, up to the estate tax exemption amount. Once inside this trust, the assets are free from estate taxes for the life of the trust. Therefore, this trust may allow you to pass along additional money to a beneficiary in excess of the estate tax exemption amount established. Another type of trust, known as a dynasty trust, allows you to transfer assets to relatives who are at least two generations younger than yourself (such as your grandchildren). A qualified personal residence trust allows you to remove the value of a home or vacation property from your estate. Each of these trusts, as well as others such as life insurance trusts, are complex in nature and require specific legal advice in determining whether they may benefit your unique situation. However, trusts offer creative estate-planning options to help you avoid taxation in many instances.

Not everyone, of course, will benefit from a trust, and costs are involved in establishing these entities. As a general rule, individuals with more than $100,000 in assets and/or substantial real estate holdings may want to consider these options and seek professional advice. Likewise, people who want to define a specific way in which heirs may receive a distribution of assets may also find trusts to be ideal. Trusts can also provide protection from lawsuits and creditor actions in some cases. Regardless of your specific needs, trusts and tax planning are often significant strategies involved in estate planning. Because of the complexities involved in their structures and estate law, legal expertise is required in order to attain solid advice on how you need to proceed.

As evident from the descriptions in this chapter, estate planning involves much more than a will. Several decisions should be made concerning how assets should be distributed after your death through estate planning. At the same time, choices concerning healthcare decisions, management of business affairs, tax strategies, and the administration of your will remain important components. These considerations apply to everyone regardless of the size of the estate, but for individuals with larger amounts of assets, such planning becomes even more critical. Likewise, the nuances associated with many of these estate-planning features can be rather complex and confusing. As a result, three pieces of advice are provided. First, seek competent financial and legal counseling when pursuing estate planning. Secondly, do not procrastinate when it comes to estate planning. And third, review and revise your estate planning strategies regularly. Through these actions, you will more likely ensure your wishes are realized and your estate will be maximally protected.

CHAPTER 10

Conclusion

As you are likely now aware, planning for your retirement is anything but simple. However, breaking down various components of retirement planning allows you to better understand the various opportunities and options available to you. The information you now have regarding retirement strategies allows you to better communicate with other financial and legal experts concerning your own specific retirement plan. It allows you to more thoroughly assess whether you are pursuing the opportunities that will give you the best chance to reach your retirement goals. The more knowledge you have concerning retirement options and strategies, the more likely you can devise a plan that aligns with your ultimate dreams. This book hopefully has provided a strong foundation in that regard.

While some financial sites define affluent households as those having a certain level of annual income, affluence from the perspective of retirement planning involves other considerations. For example, strategies that seek to protect your assets and income streams now and into the future are features of affluent households. Likewise, estate planning and making provisions to assist your children and parents in their future needs are also attributed to affluent households. Retirement planning is, therefore, much more than simply identifying retirement income sources for later life. It involves many other areas, as described in this book, and these combine to facilitate the ability to become a truly affluent household in retirement.

As noted, diversification is an important strategy when it comes to planning for retirement. In addition to traditional retirement vehicles such as 401(k)s, IRAs, and pensions, utilizing investments in annuities, stocks, and bonds offer other avenues for investment growth for future retirement income. Real estate options also exist, ranging from your home's equity to rental property income, real estate investment opportunities, and reverse mortgages. Finally, a solid understanding of Social Security income alternatives, including your optimal retirement age, helps to coordinate this source of retirement income with other income sources. Each of these income sources has its own set of inherent risks and benefits; by having a diversified portfolio of these sources, you will be better able to predict your actual retirement income in the future.

Prioritization of investments according to their tax features remains an important overall strategy in evaluating various opportunities for retirement investments. Remember, free money offers the best option when it comes to retirement income. Matching retirement funds received from employers represents an example of free money, and you should always seek to maximize these opportunities. Secondly, tax-free money represents the next best option for retirement income investments, while tax-deferred growth investments represent the third best option. That these investment sources should be explored before considering taxable options is a general rule. Even if all the details of an investment opportunity are lacking, you can often streamline your investment choices according to these prioritization rules, and this can help guide you in asking the right questions and making the best decisions.

Finally, nothing can replace sound, effective, expert advice when it comes to retirement planning. Let's face it: retirement planning can be complicated. While the chapters in this book have provided solid insights into essential components of thorough retirement planning, the information is by no means comprehensive. Seek expert help utilizing professionals who have the right level of education and experience for the task at hand. For example, seek advice from an attorney when it comes to estate planning needs and legal issues rather than seeking guidance from a financial advisor alone. As an attorney, financial advisor, and insurance specialist, I am aware of how each area of expertise offers important guidance related to specific areas of retirement planning. Use the knowledge you have gained to help you select the right professional for the needs you have.

In summary, key strategies that have been encouraged throughout this book include asset and income diversification, investment prioritization, knowledge acquisition, and expert assistance. Yet each of these will have a limited impact if you fail to commit to a retirement plan and act according to the steps of the plan you adopt. Unfortunately, these shortcomings in planning and commitment occur all too often, and couples can later realize their dreams for retirement cannot be realized as a result. However, even if you are in your fifties, constructing a retirement plan today can still benefit you greatly in most instances. Armed with a solid foundation of knowledge about various retirement planning concepts and strategies, taking that first step toward your own retirement plan will likely be much easier. For those of you who have already taken that step, refining your plan based on this knowledge should be more easily accomplished. So, what are you waiting for? Plan your dream retirement today and start investing in your future.

Make it happen! ☺

About the Author

David Hollander is the founder and CEO of Liberty Group. He is considered a trusted voice in advising Californians on ways to protect their assets. An elder law attorney and investment advisor for more than thirty years, he has assisted thousands of persons with increasing income, lowering taxation, preserving principal, and maximizing assets.

David also is the host of the *Protect Your Assets* radio show, which airs on KNBR AM 680, KSFO AM 560, KLAA AM 830, and KNEWS 94.3.

He also authored the book *The Entrepreneur's Exit Strategy*. He has a bachelor's degree from the University of California, Berkeley, and a law degree from the University of San Diego School of Law.

OAKLAND
411 30th Street, Second Floor
Oakland, CA 94609
Phone: 510.658.1880

NEWPORT BEACH
4675 MacArthur Court, Suite 590
Newport Beach, CA 92660
Phone: 949.504.8673

LARKSPUR
485 Magnolia Avenue
Larkspur, CA 94939
Phone: 415.229.9002

Email: retire@libertygroupllc.com
Web: libertygroupllc.com

Scan for Website and Social Media